THE VINCE LOMBARDI STORY

Books by Dave Klein

Great Moments in Baseball

Great Moments in Golf

The Vince Lombardi Story

THE VINCE LOMBARDI STORY

by Dave Klein

New York • Lion Books • 1971

To the memory of Vince Lombardi,
and for the millions who admired him

CONTENTS

PHOTOGRAPHS

F O R E W O R D

SHORTLY AFTER THE DEATH OF VINCE LOMBARDI, Dave Klein came to me with the request to write the foreword for this biography of the man. I must say I viewed the proposal with mixed emotions.

Vince was my friend, my dear friend, and the loss we all suffered was still overpowering and fresh. I was hesitant at first, thinking there were others equally capable of remembering this unique man; indeed, others more capable than I.

But I have decided to do this, in the hope that I will be able to express in the public print my admiration for Vince and my remembrances of this close and intensely loyal friend, as well as my deep personal relationship with him. I trust all those who loved him, and who were fortunate to have claimed him as a friend, will understand, and remember with me.

I knew Vince for nearly forty years. We were classmates at Fordham University in 1933, and through all the years that followed I found there were several men named Vince Lombardi. He was not intense and moody all the time, but more so than any other man I've known. He loved to laugh, and he loved to talk football. He was a more than able coach, as we all know, and I have often suspected that it was due to his love of teaching and his driving pursuit of knowledge from those he respected professionally.

Vince was deeply religious, and he was a dedicated family man, two qualities I have always held in the highest respect. He was also a profoundly proud man, and for this people looked upon him with a touch of awe. He took each setback, however small, as a personal affront, and always vowed to reverse the outcome the next time. He truly believed there would always be a "next time."

As I have said, I first met Vince at Fordham, although during our undergraduate days we did not have a particularly close relationship. We said hello as we passed daily on the campus and in the halls, and although he knew my father's position as the owner of the New York Giants, he never brought it up in our conversations.

We became much closer when he returned to Fordham as an assistant coach some years later, for we found we had a mutual friend, Father Kevin O'Brien, who was the faculty moderator of athletics at the university. By then I had graduated and had begun working for the Giants, as the team secretary. But I always kept close to the school.

The Giants planned to train one summer in Superior, Wisconsin, and I invited the Fordham coaching staff to spend ten days with us there. Not all of them could come, but two, along with Father O'Brien, did—Jimmy Noble, another assistant, and Vince. It was there that I first heard him laugh, a deep, distinctive, hearty laugh. We used to sit out on the veranda of the dormitory after dinner, telling stories into the evening. I remember Vince loved the tales told by our head scout, Jack Lavelle. Vince was Jack's greatest audience.

That summer was the first time I really got to know him, and we maintained our friendship for all the subsequent years. We spoke often, even more so when we were angry with each other. That happened occasionally, just as you will have more fights with your brother than with a stranger. But we never got angry enough to stop talking.

When Vince was coaching under Colonel "Red" Blaik at Army, we were training the Giants at Bear Mountain State Park, not far from the Military Academy. Vince would drive down in the evenings to visit. He impressed our coach, Steve Owen, with his knowledge and his curiosity. He was always thinking of ways to improve the game, always seeking something new, something different.

I remember one summer, when Vince was the backfield coach at West Point, he became involved in a particularly ticklish situation with Blaik. The team's quarterback was Bobby Blaik, Red's son, and Vince was his coach. I think it was 1950. Anyway, Vince had gotten fascinated by a new way of snapping the ball from center—with a little twist, so that the quarterback would get the ball crosswise, ready to grip the laces and throw or hand off. This was contradictory to the way Blaik had taught, and he was slow to accept any radical change from his young assistant. But what made Red even more reluctant was the concern that a new style of play, a change of basic fundamentals, might impair his son's progress, and Red always needed a smoothly functioning quarterback.

Well, we were sitting in the dining room up there, the Cub Room, I think. It was crowded. Vince was trying to explain to us what he meant. He wanted to convince us that the extra turn of the hand wouldn't slow up the snap. "Look," he bellowed, slapping his forehead excitably, "I can hit myself with the side of my hand as fast as with the palm. Look." And there he was, while all the other diners in the room watched dumbfounded, slapping himself repeatedly in the head.

I think that sold Steve on his qualities right there, for after that he always predicted greatness in coaching for Vince. I think I also made up my mind that if the opportunity ever arose, I wanted Vince to be with the Giants. I felt we could use his fresh thinking, his new ideas, as well as his dedication and intensity.

Then, late in the 1953 season, we had decided to replace Owen the following season. I went to West Point with my brother Jack, who was president of the Giants, and we tried to see if Blaik would want to be considered for the job. He wouldn't, but I asked if we might speak to Vince about a position as an assistant with us. I had mentioned his name to Jack earlier, and he was in full accord.

I don't honestly remember where we were when I asked Vince if he was interested. "Would you like a shot at the backfield job for the Giants?" His reaction was immediate. "Yes, I would," he said, "if we can straighten out the financial things." There were many fringe benefits for coaches at West Point, such as rent-free housing and the chance to buy in the post exchange, that had to be compensated for by the Giants. When we finally hired him, I think his first contract was in the area of $10,000, which was high for an assistant in those years.

Vince worked for us from 1954 through 1958, when he received an offer to become the head coach of the Green Bay Packers. He had one year remaining on his Giants' contract, and he came to me and asked if I would release him. His wife, Marie, didn't want him to take it. She loved New York and wanted to stay. But I couldn't stand in his way. I gave him his release, but I told him that if the head job ever opened up on the Giants, he would be the first man I would ask.

Vince had done a wonderful job for us in the five seasons he was our backfield coach, and I knew he was ready to become a head coach. In fact, several of the men who worked or played for Jim Lee Howell in that period went on to become head coaches. There was Vince, Allie Sherman, Tom Landry, Alex Webster, Dick Nolan, Bill Austin, and Harland Svare.

I remember the first time the Giants played Green Bay for the National Football League championship. It was 1961, in Green Bay. I left on the team plane. My wife, Ann, and three other New York couples, all friends of ours and of the Lombardis, flew out later. Vince met them at the airport, took them to his home, where I met them, and from there he took us out to dinner. It was the night before the game, and I guess there were about a dozen people at our table. He wouldn't talk about the next day, except to say, "I'm sure we'll play a good game." That was very important to him.

We must have sat there for three or four hours, just talking and remembering, when he looked at his watch. "I'm sorry, but it's late," he said, helping Marie to her feet. "I have to go. You're on your own." He just left, making us take cabs back to the hotel. We ribbed him about that for years.

The years passed, and Vince achieved all the glory any man could have. Then he gave up the coaching half of his duties in Green Bay and became general manager. But he itched to come back, once having left the sidelines. A few weeks before the announcement was officially made, he told me of his opportunity to join the Washington Redskins. I was pleased, and with Vince back in our division, we didn't feel quite as bad about losing our rivalry with Cleveland in the realignment of the league. With Vince in Washington, I knew there would always be an intense rivalry between our teams, which is great for football and the fans. It was worth everything to me, and the only point I insisted on was that the Giants and the Redskins stay together, no matter with which other teams we were to be grouped.

Sadly, he was there for just one season. Then he took ill, and he knew what it was and how serious it was. But he never gave up. "I'll beat it," he told me. "I'm gonna lick it yet." True to his nature, he never even discussed the cancer with Marie, although of course she knew everything. He just preferred to bear his burden alone. Ann and I went to see him after his first operation, and it was then that Marie told us how bad it really was. We went to see him again, when he was home, and while we were watching the British Open on television, he turned to me. "You know what it is, don't you?" he asked. "You know what I have?" I told him I did.

"I'll make it," he said. "I'll beat this cancer."

He never did.

The last time I saw Vince was about two weeks before the

end. He was back in the hospital, and by then we all knew it was just a matter of time. There was no question then. It had spread too fast, and it was obvious he was not going to beat it.

I went there with Alex Webster and Frank Gifford, two of the greatest runners in the history of the Giants and the two players who felt closest to Vince. We stayed for just about three minutes. That was all he could take. He was too weak. We left, and we knew we had seen him for the last time.

For as long as I live, I will consider myself a lucky man to have known Vince Lombardi. I don't think any man could have had a better, more loyal friend.

I am grateful to have known him, grateful to have worked with him, and above all, grateful that he was my friend.

A man like Vince Lombardi can never be forgotten.

WELLINGTON MARA
President, New York Giants

PREFACE

The bulletin on the Associated Press wire ticker, inescapably cold, seemed almost to scream out its news. "Vince Lombardi dead at fifty-seven," it said, on the morning of September 3, 1970.

While the death of this man came as a shock to football fans everywhere, it affected those who knew him even more profoundly. He was a vital and dynamic man, and a legend of invincibility had grown up around him. He had about him an aura of fire and steel, unbending and unyielding. Surely, this was the man who could continue, who could fight back, the man who would yet achieve the goals of his perfectionist's ego.

But no. Cancer came, then death. And it claimed much more than a man.

Lombardi, more than any other coach, changed the face of professional football. He did it by the simple and yet impossible act of forcing his will upon other men, lifting them beyond what they knew they could do, above what they accepted as their limits. He did it his way, convinced that it was the only sensible way, and then he went on to prove that he had been right. He became the epitome of despotism, and his image was that of a callous dictator. But there was more emotion in Vince Lombardi than anyone outside knew.

"As a person," he once said, "I am just not well enough adjusted to accept a loss. The trouble with me is that my ego cannot accept defeat." He drove himself harder and with more fury than he did his players, and yet his players were driven well past what other coaches and other athletes considered to be the bounds of tolerance.

In attempting to explain his conditioning and teaching theories, he said: "If I find a boy with talent, I feel that it is his
moral obligation to fulfill it, and I will not relent on my own
responsibility to him. Sometimes he won't even be aware of
the talent he possesses, which serves only to make my job that
much more difficult."

As a sportswriter for *The Newark Star-Ledger* during the
time of Vince Lombardi's head-coaching career, I came into
contact with him several times, and in my mind's eye there are
innumerable reflections, countless impressions of this man. He
was honest to the point of rudeness. His directness sometimes
caused him to snap back at interviewers, often embarrassing
them, but he was not cruel. "You are a professional," he once
said, "as I am a professional. If we cannot function together
on a professional level, I do not have the time to function with
you at all."

The day Vince Lombardi died, I was in my newsroom. As
is the practice of newspapers, I had been asked to prepare an
obituary weeks earlier, when it became clear how serious his
illness was. I had written the obit, nearly six typewritten pages
of it, and it had been set in type and shelved for the day when
it would be needed.

Then he died, and I secured a galley proof of the obit to
make final corrections, adding the time of death and the
funeral arrangements. But I had written that obit when Vince
Lombardi was still alive, and I suppose I never really believed
he could be dying. I asked for permission to rewrite, and aside
from the historical facts and dates, I used nothing of the first
version. The obituary that was published was written with
emotion, with a sense of deep loss.

Toward the end of Lombardi's tenure in Green Bay, he had
come to call me by my first name. Perhaps he thought I had
then been around long enough. I cannot forget, even now, how
good it felt that first time. He was my friend, and I miss him.

Many men were closer to him. I know these men, too, and

they have been gracious enough to reveal to me the depth of their relationships with Vince Lombardi. That is why this is more than a biography; it is a series of recollections, an anthology of Vince Lombardi told by those who knew him best.

Traditionally, newspaper reporters are supposed to be detached. We scowl at one of our own caught cheering in the press box. We are said to be callous, to indulge in irreverent, black humor on the most solemn occasions. But we are also human beings, and the loss of a man such as Vince Lombardi cuts deeply.

I have found, in the months since his death, that I am left with many of his thoughts. "Pain," he said, "is only in the mind. You can tell yourself it does not hurt, and it will not." The pain of his loss is not just in the mind. It is in the heart, and there it remains.

When I had decided that I wanted to write this book, I wrote a far-from-professional statement. "It was a personal honor to have experienced a friendship with this man, and it would stand as a personal honor to write his story."

Now I have the chance. I only hope he would have approved.

For help in preparing this book, I would like to express my gratitude to Wellington Mara, Don Smith, Jim Lee Howell, Alex Webster, Frank Gifford, Kyle Rote, Jim Garrett, Norb Hecker, Emlen Tunnell, Jim Hitchcock, my brother, Moss, Harold Rosenthal, Chuck Lane, Joe Blair, Jim Heffernan, and two very special people, my wife, Carole, who missed more than her share of meals and movies, and my mother, who put her teaching background to its most severe test.

THE VINCE LOMBARDI STORY

Block of Granite

AT FIRST, VINCE LOMBARDI WANTED TO BE A PRIEST. BUT
it didn't work out. Then he thought becoming a prize fighter
was a good idea. It wasn't.

"I just didn't have the dedication to enter the clergy," he
once said. "I couldn't do it. I have more respect for those people than any other in the world. I just couldn't measure up to
their standards, and it is something I have often regretted."

As for the manly art of self-defense, Lombardi remembered
with a smile. "I fought one bout, in the Golden Gloves. I won
it, too. But I didn't like the idea of getting hit, and I am not
so sure I enjoyed the idea of hitting other men, either. So I
gave up that ambition. After that, I more or less gravitated to
football."

Vincent Thomas Lombardi was born on June 11, 1913, the
first of the five children of Henry Lombardi, who had emigrated
from Italy to the Sheepshead Bay section in Brooklyn, New
York, and his American-born wife, Matilda Izzo Lombardi.

After two years at Brooklyn's Cathedral Prep, the young Lombardi transferred to Saint Francis Prep, where he starred as a fullback on the football team. The priesthood given up, he decided to concentrate on academics and athletics. "I had this drive," he often said, "to be first, or best, in everything. I wasn't born with much size or speed, and so everything I did in the field of athletics was a struggle. I had to try harder than anyone else because I didn't want to fail again. But there is something to be said for that kind of an attitude, because I found that if I really wanted something badly enough, it was possible. I always tried to want it more than the other kids. That was my edge. It was the only one I had, so I had to work with it, to make it work for me."

Football, then, entered Lombardi's life early on, and though he made several attempts to discard it, the game stuck. He had played well enough at Saint Francis Prep to win him a football scholarship to Fordham University in the Bronx. At the time, the New York college was a nationally renowned football power as well as one of the country's most demanding academic institutions. Throughout the 1930's and 1940's, it was a rare season indeed when the Fordham Rams were not contending for national, or at least eastern, supremacy.

Lombardi became a guard, and the line he played on was dubbed "the Seven Blocks of Granite." He was 5 feet 8 inches tall and weighed 185 pounds, and the coaching staff at Fordham was immediately impressed with his intensity.

Frank Leahy, who went on to become the master coach at the University of Notre Dame, was the line coach at Fordham during the 1934–37 period, when Lombardi was an undergraduate.

"Vince Lombardi was one of the Seven Blocks of Granite during my years as line coach at Fordham," Leahy says today, "and it just might be that he was responsible for the birth of the Seven Blocks legend. I always considered it a personal honor to have known this young Italian warrior. Even then,

Vince was special and unusual in that he always managed to extract more than he really had to give. He had very few God-given talents. He wasn't large, not very fast, but he always displayed a burning desire to win, to excel. At all times he was willing to pay any price, which included effort, blood, pain, and sacrifice. His leadership abilities were on display even at that early point in his young life. He was, really, an inspiration to the rest of the team."

The six other members of the Seven Blocks were Leo Paquin and John Druze, ends; Ed Franco and Al Barbatsky, tackles; Alex Wojciechowicz at center; and Nat Pierce was the second guard. The team also included Russ Monica, a reserve guard who later became an outstanding player, and Hugh Addonizio, a quarterback who went on to become mayor of New Jersey's largest city, Newark.

"I look back at Fordham," Leo Paquin says today, "and I guess what strikes me is that there was no one special thing about him. He had no halo over his head, nothing that really set him apart from everybody else. If you take four categories —athletics, academics, religion, and character—you wouldn't have put Vinnie first in any of them. But what you'd begin to notice is that he was among the top two or three in each category. Somebody else's name might appear ahead of him in one or two of the categories, but he was up there in all of them. We just didn't notice it then. He was just one of the boys."

Alex Wojciechowicz, elected to the Pro Football Hall of Fame in Canton, Ohio, after an all-pro career with the Detroit Lions and Philadelphia Eagles, remained a close friend of Lombardi's throughout the years. He wept openly at the news of Vince's death, and shortly afterward he, too, recalled their college days for an interviewer.

"He was an inspiration to all of us. He was what we called a fighting guard in those days. Vince was a battler who would not take any guff from anybody. He was a perfectionist, and he never made a mistake that hurt the team. He was a senior when I was a junior, and he gave us—me—great confidence. We always sang on the bus going to our games, and Vince always led us. He had two favorite songs, 'Regina Coeli Laetare' and 'The Fordham Ram.' The 'Ram' ends with 'we'll do or die,' and he meant that. God, did he mean it! And he made us mean it, and believe it, too. We would stare straight into the eyes of our opponents across the line of scrimmage and he'd say: 'We're ready to die; are you?' "

During Lombardi's college days, Fordham had two head coaches. One was Frank Cavanaugh, a man of steel and fire they called "the Iron Major." The other was "Sleepy Jim" Crowley, already immortalized as one of the "Four Horsemen" backfield at Notre Dame. He learned from both. Both were religious family men, proud of their country and their schools and motivated by a respect for tradition and principle.

"Most of the boys were great believers in discipline," Crowley once said. "It was instilled in them by their families. But I could easily see that Vince was special. He never wavered from his goals. He always gave his best, and he did not hesitate to chew out other players, even older than he, if he thought they were loafing."

"In those days," Leahy recalls, "football was not as commercial as it later became. We played it for the satisfaction of bringing in our school a winner, and for personal satisfaction. It was manly combat, for a good cause.

"You had to eat with it and sleep with it; you had to live it. It must be difficult for some kids today to understand how we felt, but Fordham football was not an individual thing. We played for the team, for the school. We could never shrug off a loss, because it was a great catastrophe. That's how deeply we felt about our football. We sacrificed our individuality in order to make the larger contribution to the team. I've been told this is how Vince coached when he got to the Packers, with that thought in mind. Well, he learned it at Fordham."

Leahy remembers Lombardi's early determination. "He was more intense than any of them. He considered it a personal affront when a play worked against us, or when one of ours failed to work. He had a flash-point temper, and sometimes it got away from him. It affected his concentration, but you could see him fighting *that,* too."

"Like my father before me," Lombardi once commented, "I have a violent temper with which I have been struggling all my life, and with which I have had to effect a compromise. It is unavoidable, but it must not be irrational. I have tried all my life to leash the outbursts of my temper, not simply to waste it in anger."

Lombardi was graduated summa cum laude from Fordham in 1937, just as the nation was beginning to emerge from the ravages of the Great Depression that started in 1929. But jobs were still scarce, and jobs that paid well were nonexistent. There was nothing out there for Lombardi to do, and so he fulfilled a latecoming desire to enter law. He applied for admission to the Fordham Law School, was accepted, and attended classes for two years. But he did not finish, leaving, instead, to marry.

Now finding employment became essential, and Vince turned to teaching. He accepted a position at Saint Cecilia High School in Englewood, New Jersey, where he not only coached the basketball and football teams but also taught Latin, physics, and chemistry. The salary wasn't much—"They paid me seventeen hundred dollars a year for all that," he was to recall years later—but the life was satisfying. During the summers Lombardi worked as the foreman of a New Jersey highway construction crew and drove a truck. Yet he found time to earn credits for a master's degree in education at Seton Hall University in South Orange.

"There was fun in coaching then that I have not found since," Lombardi said nearly two decades later, "and certainly cannot find now. Everything was a struggle, and Marie and I were as close as a husband and wife could ever be. We worked hard to make small gains. We knocked ourselves out for whatever we received, and it was that much more satisfying because of it. Of course, I'm a bit more well-paid now, but the pressures of this job are too much for any one man." He was then head coach and general manager of the Packers; as general manager he was acting virtually as team president. "There is no way I could ever get as much pure delight from coaching again, not the kind I found at Saint Cecilia High."

In all, Lombardi spent eight years there, and his football and basketball teams won six state championships. His coaching philosophy had already gone past the embryonic stages.

"I guess I was always tough," he said. "But it was the way I had to be. It came naturally. I had to drive athletes to make them perform as well as I knew they could. When I got to professional football, I simply turned up the volume."

"Red" Gerrity, who was basketball coach at nearby Englewood High School, became one of Lombardi's closest friends. "We went out together, to dinner with our wives, to lunch by ourselves. We spent several New Year's Eves together. We traded ideas on coaching and on the problems of the world. We really were close friends. But that old son-of-a-gun was the toughest competitor I ever met. During the week before the Saint Cecilia-Englewood basketball game, he wouldn't speak to me, not even in church."

By the end of World War II, Lombardi was evaluating his career and his future. "I was in my thirties, and I was still a high school coach. I had learned by then that coaching was what I wanted to do, and if that was the case, I decided I had better try to advance myself. I didn't think I'd be satisfied remaining a high school teacher, and a part-time coach. A job had opened at Fordham, and I applied for it. I got it, too."

It was in 1947 that Vince Lombardi became an assistant coach at his alma mater.

"I remember being worried about that move. Was I really

cut out to be a coach? I mean, high school is one thing, because you are teaching at the same time, and there is really no pressure on a high school coach. But at Fordham it was more intense. Winning was very important, and while it was not as important, say, as building men, it had become traditional that the team won. I wondered if I had the tools to be a part of all that. I was afraid of failing. I always have been."

Leo Paquin, the end on the Seven Blocks of Granite line, had no doubts that Lombardi would succeed. "Vinnie was the ideal man for coaching," he remembers. "He was dedicated to the concepts of coaching. Not many men were as emotional as he, but his was purely natural. Some coaches turn it on and off, and after a while the players notice and that coach becomes less believable. But Lombardi was always honest, always blunt, and always turned on to the highest volume."

Paquin, too, went into coaching after graduation, and there were times when he took his teams from Saint Francis Xavier in New York City onto the field against those of Saint Cecilia. "He never gave me a smile or an inch," Paquin says. "I never expected it, either. That's the kind of a man he was."

In 1947, Lombardi coached the Fordham freshman team. In 1948, he was moved up to the varsity as an assistant.

"When I look back on those years," he was to say much later, "I am amazed to realize just how little I really knew, both about football and about men. But I was happy with the life of a coach, because I loved football and I loved teaching. I am sure some amount of ego enters this picture, because a man must have a good image of himself. Nothing can make it grow as much as success."

In 1949, an assistant coach at West Point, Sid Gillman, accepted the head coaching job at the University of Cincinnati. That event was crucial for Vince Lombardi.

He was introduced to the Colonel—Earl "Red" Blaik, head football coach for the United States Military Academy at West Point.

There would grow between these two men a profound relationship, which continued to Lombardi's death. He often expressed his love for Blaik and his respect for him as a coach and a tactician. "Nobody knew anything about football unless they knew the Colonel," Lombardi often repeated. "He was as great a teacher as I have ever known. He took me in and taught me everything I know. Not only football, but life, and how to handle men, and how to win. Even how to lose, although I admit I never learned that well at all."

Both men were tough. Both were stern disciplinarians. Both were devoted to the sport of football and its proper execution. Both were football fundamentalists. Both extracted far more from ordinary athletes than those athletes ever suspected was there. Both, too, were emotional, high-strung, and easily excitable men, men to whom the right play at the right time became sufficient to justify an entire season of strenuous work.

"I had never heard of Vince Lombardi when Gillman told me he was leaving," Blaik remembers. "It happened rather suddenly, and I was at a loss as to who might become Sid's replacement. I started receiving applications in the mail, but I have never held much with applications. They were too impersonal. Finally, a friend of mine, Tim Cohane, told me about this young fellow who had done such a good job with the Fordham freshmen. Timmy thought this guy was just great, and I said I would talk to Lombardi as a favor to him. I never expected anything would come of it.

"So he came up to the Point and we sat down in my office, and in just a few minutes I knew Lombardi was different. Maybe it was just a hunch, I don't know, but there was a look about him. He seemed so eager, so determined.

"I didn't know a thing about him. I never saw him play, and I didn't even know he was one of the Seven Blocks of Granite. Yet as we were talking, I began to see that he had a good knowledge of the game, that he was imaginative, and that he could communicate with a certain excitement. You know, even then—and he was only about thirty-five or thirty-six—he had that special quality of being able to electrify a room. His eyes flashed, and he came alive when he started talking about football theory. I hired him, and I will always feel that it was one of the wisest decisions I ever made."

Blaik had come to the United States Military Academy in 1941, fresh from a brilliant coaching career at Dartmouth College, where he had taken a lackluster team and molded it into an annual contender for national honors. It was his way. Like Lombardi, Blaik earned a reputation for being a man who could make success bloom where mediocrity had been sown.

The Army teams of "Doc" Blanchard and Glenn Davis had won top national honors in 1944 and 1945. Blaik became the country's most successful, most copied coach, and Lombardi often admitted later that he did not expect to land the job.

"I really didn't have the kind of experience the Colonel wanted," he would say. "I had started late, and I hadn't had very much responsibility at that point. But something clicked between us. I have often wondered what might have happened to me if I had not applied for that job, or had not been accepted."

Lombardi got the job, and in a short time he became Blaik's most trusted aide. "In the five seasons Vince spent with me at West Point," the Colonel says, "I'll bet we must have spent three or four thousand hours looking at game films. It is the only way to really learn football. That plus long hours."

Lombardi was developing now, absorbing the theory and strategy Blaik was force-feeding into him. For, as with Lombardi himself later, when Blaik found a young man with real potential, he would be a merciless teacher.

"I'd walk into the office at eight in the morning," Lombardi said, "and without so much as saying 'good morning' he would start on me. 'It's third down. The ball is on your thirty. You need four yards. They are in a seven-man defense with the halfback playing up close behind the strong side. What play will you call? Why? Defend it.' The man never stopped thinking about football. He was a perfectionist.

"That's a key word in coaching, you know. Perfectionist. The satisfactions are few for such men, but I've never known a good coach who wasn't one. You don't do things right once in a while; you do them right all the time."

Lombardi's relationship with Blaik deepened. Later, when Vince was the Packers' head coach, he was in almost weekly telephone contact with his since-retired mentor. "Sometimes," Blaik recalls, "he'd be down, or he'd be confused or under that pressure, and he'd call me to ask what he should do. But he never really wanted advice. He just wanted to talk, to unload on someone, and he felt he could talk to me. I've never known a man who blamed himself so much for the failings of the players. He thought he could make any athlete a great one, and when he couldn't, he blamed himself. If a player didn't give one hundred percent, Vince felt he had failed as a coach."

At the Point, there were hard work and long hours, often as many as eighteen a day. "He learned quickly," Blaik says. "In a few years, he was able to guess my next move. We'd come up with the same solution to a game problem on the sidelines at the same time. I suppose it could be said that I did a good teaching job, but I wouldn't have had the same success with many other men. Vince Lombardi was born to coach football, and I just had the good fortune to be his instructor. After a while, he could have taught me. But I never let on to that. No, sir."

In Jerry Kramer's book *Lombardi: Winning Is the Only Thing*, Blaik described Lombardi's first day of spring practice in 1949. Vince was the offensive line coach, for a team that would go through the season undefeated, averaging forty points a game.

"I remember that day. He was standing near me, talking about a minor detail on the practice schedule. Suddenly somebody in his group, one of the linemen, did something wrong.

The linemen were probably seventy-five feet away, and he dashed over there, screaming at the top of his lungs. I yelled 'Vince, Vince,' and he pulled up short, like a charging horse. He was explosive. He had a short fuse. Of course, he was still immature. That was really his only shortcoming when he first joined us. He didn't have the control of his emotions he later acquired. His attitude at the beginning, I think, was 'they're all equal; let's give 'em all hell.'

"At first the boys didn't understand him. They didn't understand his drive. But he could overcome his immaturity because he had such a dynamic personality, so much youthful vitality. And, like me, he was captivated by the game. Once he got to playing around with circles and *X*'s, he was in another world. This is the one thing about football that ordinary laymen don't understand at all. There's nothing comparable to the fascination of developing a football team. I'm not thinking about the games. It's how do you approach a season? A game? How do you get the most out of your material? How do you adjust your material to that of the opponent? How do you make the intelligent move, the decisive move, always under that tremendous pressure?

"The possibilities are endless, and a man with as inquisitive and searching a mind as Vince's could see those possibilities and could devote a lifetime to coping with them."

In 1950, when the infamous "cribbing scandal" broke at West Point, Blaik's son Bob, the team's quarterback, was one of those expelled for allegedly cheating on exams. "It was an asinine thing," Blaik says. "They harmed a lot of young boys, those antifootball people at the academy, and they harmed the Military Academy, too. Next to me, Vince was probably the most deeply affected person. Everything we had built and everything we stood for went flying right out the window in twenty-four hours. He, like myself, never forgave the people up there who forced and magnified the whole situation."

The team was nearly wiped out by the expulsions, and the

proud cadets were forced to face a rugged national schedule with, as Blaik remembers, "a rinky-dink team." They won only two games in 1951, and only four the following season. Then, early in 1953, the cadets journeyed to Northwestern and just lost in the closing minutes. It might have been a memorable, emotion-charged upset. Blaik recalls Lombardi's reaction to the game: "He sat in the dressing room afterward and cried, because one player had made a mistake that cost the game for a bunch of kids who had worked so hard to come from nowhere. It must have made an impression on the team, because we didn't lose again that season. We went on to become eastern champions, and Vince was even more proud of those boys than he was of our undefeated team in nineteen forty-nine. And so was I."

Blaik was beginning to consider retirement, and he says "there was no doubt that Vince would have been my successor had he stayed at West Point. He certainly was my able assistant in nineteen fifty-four. But the New York Giants came calling. First, they asked me if I would take their head coaching job, because Steve Owen had retired, and they needed a new man with a reputation. I turned them down, and then Wellington Mara [at that time a team vice president; he became president at the death of his older brother, John V. Mara] asked me if he could talk to Vince. He wanted to get him as an assistant. I hated to lose him, and Vince didn't like the idea of leaving, because he always had tremendous loyalty. But he had to take the offer, of course. He couldn't turn down an opportunity with the New York Giants and professional football."

Lombardi later confessed to second thoughts. "The main attraction of the National Football League," he said, in explaining his decision to leave West Point and the Colonel, "was the quality of the players. Some of them didn't know how good they were, but they were all superb athletes, or they wouldn't have been holding down jobs in that kind of a league. That's true of any group of professionals. You'll find those who achieve the most are those who put their talent to better use, and there's no way to escape the necessity of hard work, long hours, and personal dedication.

"I decided to go with the pros because I felt I could come closer to finding the perfect football player. College students are great to work with, especially the sort you find at the military academies, and they provided me with many great moments. But many of them are just not equipped to become outstanding athletes. Professionals are—or they should be, at any rate. The lure was fascinating. I would be working with more mature, more gifted football players. I don't think I had any other choice, being the kind of a man I am."

It was 1954 when Vince Lombardi hit the pros. He never stopped hitting.

Five Seasons with the Giants

IN 1954, THE NEW YORK GIANTS UNDERWENT SEVERAL IN-
ternal changes. They dismissed Steve Owen, their head coach
since 1931. They replaced him with Jim Lee Howell, a tower-
ing man who had been an end for the team from 1937 through
1942 and then from 1946 through 1948, after the end of
World War II.

At the time when the Mara brothers—Jack and Wellington
—decided a change was necessary, Owen had three assistants
on the squad, Howell, Allie Sherman, and Ed Kolman. Kolman
was the only one not involved in the competition for the job.

The Maras had hoped to lure Red Blaik from West Point.
But Blaik turned them down, although he had been an un-
official adviser to the Giants for many years and consented to
continue in that capacity. He did not want to leave the Point.
Blaik had no more worlds to conquer, had nothing else left to
prove.

"We told Howell and Sherman at the end of the nineteen

fifty-three season that a new man was going to be named,"
Wellington Mara recalls now. "We told them they would both
be considered, and we also told them we were going to ask
Blaik first. If he took the job, that was final. I told them it
would be unfair of me to guarantee their jobs under a new
coach, for it would be difficult to saddle a new man with un-
familiar assistants. Head men are always given the option of
bringing in their own staff. I promised both Jim Lee and Allie
that if they were not retained, I would make sure to pay up
any remaining time on their contracts. I also told them that if
one of them got the job, I hoped the other would stay.

"Jim Lee said he would, but Allie said he did not see how he
could. Well, when Blaik turned us down, Jack and I thought
about the situation for a long time. We finally decided that
Jim Lee had more experience, and I called him. I asked him
if he could come over and talk to me. It was just before
Christmas of nineteen fifty-three, and he had his car packed
for the trip home to Lone Oak, Arkansas. He came in, and
I told him he had the job. He accepted it right there."

"I did have one thing to saddle Jim Lee with," he says now
with a smile. "I told him I had invited Vince Lombardi to
become an assistant. I told him I didn't know what duties
Vince might assume, but that I wanted him on the staff. Jim
Lee agreed to that, and asked if I could have Lombardi visit
with him after New Year's down in Arkansas."

Shortly after the first of the year, Lombardi flew to Arkansas.
There he and Howell spent a week together, talking football
and talking about Lombardi's duties. Sherman had decided
not to stay, and had accepted a head coaching job with Winni-
peg in the Canadian Football League. Lombardi would take
over the offensive backfield.

Vince returned to New York and met with Mara. "I don't
think I made a very good impression on my new boss," he said.
"I referred to his town as Lonesome Oaks, and when I first

arrived, he was out plowing the fields or something. I didn't
know a darned thing about farming."

But Lombardi did know a thing or two about football, and
Howell telephoned Mara shortly after the visit to say he was
delighted with the addition to his staff. "I think," he said, "that
this man will have a great future with us." Mara agreed.

Howell was a tough man, a World War II marine, and he
instantly took to Lombardi, who was, perhaps, his equal for
mental toughness and self-discipline. "We both had a love for
the basics and the fundamentals of football," Jim Lee, now the
Giants' director of personnel, remembers. "Other coaches
might like to fly off the handle, start fooling around with
fanciness and frills. But I always believed in basics. I always
felt that properly executed plays, simple and easy to work,
could win if the material was good. Vince felt that way, too.
It was a pleasure working with him, although there were times
when I was scared he would absolutely destroy some of the
players. They just weren't used to working as hard as Vince
worked them. But they saw the advantages to doing things our
way when they began to win."

One player who learned but too well what that meant was
Jimmy Garrett. In 1971, Garrett himself was an assistant
coach with the Giants under Alex Webster, a fullback in Lombardi's days who in time became the team's head coach. As
a coach, Garrett is recognized to be in the Lombardi mold—
intense, bright, imaginative, likely to have a team of his own
to run one day. But in 1956 he was a not-quite-good-enough
running back with the Giants.

"I had been hurt badly," Garrett recalls "I had broken my
leg in six places and dislocated the ankle, too. So I spent a
long time on the inactive roster, and that killed me. Lombardi
knew how badly I wanted to get back on the team, and one day,
near the end of the season, he came to me in the locker room.
We were on the way to an Eastern Conference championship,

and each game was tremendously important. The backs were wearing down from overwork. They were near exhaustion.

" 'Jimmy,' he said, 'I need help. I know you're hurt, and I know you haven't played in a long time. I know your timing is gone and you don't have any strength in that leg. But I need a favor. We're just dead from fatigue in the backfield. Webster and [Frank] Gifford and [Mel] Triplett are all beat up. I can't send them through another long practice session without some help. Will you work with us today? I know it won't be easy, and I'm not expecting much. I just need a body to put in there so we can run through the plays. Okay?' "

"I would have done anything for that man, and anything to get back on the field," Garrett continues, "and so I said I would do it. I was excited. Well, we went out to the field and I set up at a halfback position, and my leg was tight and stiff. I couldn't set down properly, but he had told me it wouldn't matter. So Charlie Conerly started calling signals for the first play, when all of a sudden I hear Lombardi scream: 'Hey, you. What kind of a stance is that? You look like a turkey. Get that leg in. Bend it. Get your behind down. You look like a fool.'

"I looked around, curious to see who was getting ripped up like that, and then I saw that he was looking right at me. I just couldn't believe it. He was like another person. He was yelling and screaming and his face turned all crimson, and he kept shaking that finger at me. You know, I tucked in my leg and I bent it, and I did it all the right way. He was right. Pain is in your mind. He never let up on me all through that practice, though. Finally, one of the linemen came over and said: 'Hey, Garrett, why don't you go run on the sidelines so he'll stop yelling at the rest of us?'

"After practice, he walked over to me in the locker room and apologized. He really looked terrible. 'I'm sorry, Jim. I don't know what happened to me. I just can't stop myself when I see something not being done right. I should have left you alone. I know you were hurt.' But he was right. He was a man always striving for perfection, and seeing me stick out there like a sore thumb just turned him on. I've never known a man like him, and in the short time I spent with him he made a deep impression on me.

"You know, lots of coaches have tried to do it his way. They've gone to all the yelling and screaming and rigid discipline, but it hasn't worked. You know why? Because they were forcing it. Vince was natural, and it was easy to see that. Players can spot a phony in a minute."

During Lombardi's five seasons with the Giants, the team won divisional championships in 1956 and 1958 and a league title in 1956. In 1958, against the Baltimore Colts for the NFL crown, the two teams played the first sudden-death game the league had ever had, and the Colts won, 23–17. At the time, it was described as the greatest game in the history of the NFL, and the game that firmly established professional football as a major sport with the fans and the networks.

Many of the Giants' greatest players were on that 1958 team, including most of the backfield trained by Lombardi. They included Charlie Conerly at quarterback; Webster and Triplett, fullbacks; Gifford at halfback; and Kyle Rote, flanker.

"The thing about playing for Lombardi," Alex Webster recalls, "was that he knew exactly how much you wanted to play, and then he decided it wasn't enough. He was a master salesman, a con man. He talked you into giving more, more than you had ever given in a football game before. He used different methods for different people, but it was all tailored to getting the same result—extra effort. I don't think I'll ever forget him, standing in the backfield during practices, screaming and yelling and cajoling and praising. He had a different approach for every player, and we knew it, but you had no choice but to be hypnotized by the man. Fear? No, I don't think we reacted out of fear of him, but I'll say this: I hated to come back to the locker room after we lost a game. He was sometimes out of control. It was like he felt we had let him down, or maybe that he had let us down. If we lost, we worked even harder the following week. But we didn't get a break. If we won, he worked us harder because he was afraid we'd get cocky and complacent."

Webster was named head coach of the Giants in 1969, and his approach, fittingly enough, was Lombardi's—except that he was friendlier. "I don't think you can stay completely aloof from the players," he explains. "But I do know that all the discipline and mental toughness I try to put into them comes from Coach. Playing under Jim Lee and Vince was the turning point of my career. I never knew football men could be so intense, so dedicated. I decided if it meant that much to them, there must be something in this game more than I had experienced. It was then that I began to love the sport."

Webster was one of Lombardi's favorites—an early-day Paul Hornung—because Vince saw in him all the qualities he respected, and some he envied. Webster was as tough a player as any who had ever pulled on cleats and shoulder pads. He played hurt. He played hard. He never quit. He always gave 100 percent. He never complained or tried to get out of practices or scrimmages. And he was tough.

Gino Marchetti, the Hall of Fame defensive end of the Baltimore Colts, once talked about just how tough Webster was: "You knew you had him on a tackle. You had both arms around him and you felt him starting to fall. Webster was never fast, and so you never worried about him breaking away with speed. But I don't remember ever tackling anybody stronger. You were never sure you had stopped him until you were sitting on him and the referee had blown the whistle. The man just never stopped fighting.

"You want to know something about Alex Webster? If I'm ever jumped by a dozen guys in a back alley, and if Webster is with me, I know we'll walk away from it. I know twelve guys will be stretched out on the street. I never knew anyone as tough."

But Webster knew how to enjoy himself. It was a way of easing the pressures of the game. Lombardi himself never acquired the knack of letting up, and he envied it in others. There were times when Webster treated the curfew clock with the disdain he showed a small linebacker. There were times when he was caught. And his reaction was a warm, pleasant laugh. "How much?" he would ask. "How much is the fine?"

It was this characteristic that Lombardi found so magnetic in Hornung and Max McGee, his two main revelers with the Packers. He knew they gave 100 percent on the field, and he knew they enjoyed having fun—even if he could never quite reconcile himself to their life style. Men like. Webster and Hornung and McGee became almost adopted sons. He chortled and clucked and punished, but always with some paternal glee.

Lombardi felt no glee about that 1958 championship game with Baltimore. He called it "the most disappointing moment of my years with the Giants. We had it won, and we gave it away. We had the world's championship in our hands, and we couldn't hold it. I know it must have been a thrilling, exciting game to watch, but I didn't watch it that way. I knew we were the better team. I knew we were going to win. When we didn't, I couldn't accept it. I suppose it is my personality. I am not well enough adjusted to accept a defeat. What do I remember about that game? Well, all of it, I suppose, but I thought Marchetti was great. Remember? He broke his leg late in the game, but he made them put him down on the sideline so he could watch the end of the game. He wouldn't leave the field until he knew his team had won or lost . . . that was admirable. That man always gave more than he had."

It was a revealing recollection. Lombardi might have remembered the ruthless artistry of Johnny Unitas's passes, or the powerful rushing of Alan Ameche at fullback, or the fierce defense of Sam Huff and Andy Robustelli, or the pulsating drama of Steve Myhra's game-tying field goal with just seconds remaining in regulation time. But no. He remembered the total dedication of a painfully injured man.

Frank Gifford, who is now a nationally known sportscaster, is hardly the smiling, friendly, carefree man he appears to be on the television screen. There is a streak of tough competitiveness that runs through this handsome son of southern California. He was as intense a football player as Webster, although more attuned to the glamour and frills of the game.

"Those teams we had, in the late nineteen fifties," he said, "were products of Jim Lee Howell and Vince Lombardi. We became arrogant, the kind of arrogance that a team winning championships must possess. When we took the field for a game, we knew we were going to win. We honestly felt the other team would have to be lucky to even score. We had been brainwashed by the coaches into accepting greatness as our right. When we did lose a game, we honestly believed the other team was lucky. 'If we had played our game,' we said, 'they wouldn't have even been close.' For the backs, anyway, this was Lombardi's teaching. He made us tough, tougher than the other teams."

Lombardi's obsession was conditioning. He was a tyrant on the practice field. Later on, after he had achieved greatness at Green Bay, he would remain the same. Henry Jordan, one of the outstanding Packer defensive tackles, once discussed Lombardi's passion. "There are two kinds of conditioning," he said. "The kind the other teams get and the Lombardi kind of conditioning. What is Lombardi conditioning? It's playing a full game, and not even perspiring in the fourth quarter, when the other guys are huffing and puffing, and their eyes are getting glassy. Coach sees to it that we consider sweating a sin."

"Fatigue makes cowards of us all," Lombardi said. "The harder you work, the harder it is to surrender. To play this game you must have that fire in you, and there is nothing that stokes a fire like hate. If they want to hate me, fine. I would prefer they hate the man across the line from them, but either

way, I want to build that hate. It's not fear that motivates a
football player, but hate. A hatred of losing, a hatred of being
made to look foolish, a hatred of being second best. The will
to excel and the will to win, they endure. They are far more
important than any events that occasion them. They must be
retained."

During his years with the Giants, Lombardi worked with
many fine performers in addition to Webster, Gifford, Triplett,
Rote, and Conerly. There were Don Heinrich and Bobby
Clatterbuck, quarterbacks; Phil King, fullback; Eddie Price,
halfback; offensive linemen like Rosey Brown, Bill Austin,
Jack Stroud, Ray Wietecha, Ray Beck, and the kickers Don
Chandler, Ben Agajanian, and Pat Summerall. All that involved the offense involved Lombardi. Indeed, his primary request of Jim Lee Howell during that introductory week in
Arkansas in 1954 was that the offense remain Lombardi's
domain.

"He wanted his own way on the offense," Wellington Mara
remembers. "Jim Lee told him that as long as it produced, it
would be that way. Jim Lee was a great one for delegating
authority. He certainly had the talent on his staff, people like
Lombardi and Tom Landry and Allie Sherman, and he knew
how to make the most out of such men. But underneath his
courteous exterior there was a tough, intent coach. He helped
Vince greatly."

In 1954, with the Cleveland Browns still much the class of
the NFL, the Giants finished with seven victories and five
losses, third behind Cleveland (9–3) and Philadelphia
(7–4–1). Lombardi fumed. In 1955, the Browns, with a
9–2–1 record, earned yet another Eastern Conference and
NFL title, while the Giants finished with a 6–5–1 record, again
third, this time behind Washington (8–4). Lombardi fumed.

Then came 1956, and all was right in Vince's world. The
Giants zoomed past the arch-rival Browns, who were in a down
year (finishing 5–7) and won the Eastern Conference cham-

pionship with an 8–3–1 record, scoring 264 points, allowing only 197.

"We became a team that season," Vince once offered. "All the pieces started to fit, and the players began thinking together. That was most important. They were thinking alike, and thinking like winners."

The offense was a powerhouse. Webster, Gifford, and Triplett ran roughshod over the defenses. Conerly became a complete quarterback. The receiving heroics of Bob Schnelker and Rote perfectly complemented his passing. The defense was feared throughout the league, with such as Robustelli, Harland Svare, Cliff Livingston, Bill Svoboda, Dick Nolan, Jimmy Patton, Emlen Tunnell, and Herb Rich showing the way.

The Giants slaughtered the Chicago Bears in the championship game, 47–7. The dynasty had been born, and although 1957 saw a resurgence by the Browns (the Giants were second, 7–5), New York was to dominate for most of the next half-dozen seasons.

"Lombardi had a lot to do with it," Webster says. "He never let us think we were that good. No, that's not right. He made us believe we were better than any other team, but he never let us think we were so good that we didn't have to work at it. I think he worked us harder after we started winning, because he was afraid we would let up and not win again. And again. He was a hard man, but you had to respect him. He knew what he was doing, and he proved it to us. I think he made all of us twice the players we might have been. I can't forget the sound of that voice, harping and yelling and demanding. He sure left a mark on me, I'll tell you that. Man, I couldn't go to sleep some nights without hearing that voice."

Tunnell, a member of the Pro Football Hall of Fame and one of the finest safeties to play the game, knew Vince better when he followed him to Green Bay. Emlen, one of the league's first black assistant coaches (with the Giants), recalls his impressions.

"When he was with New York, he coached the offense. So, naturally, I didn't get to work with him a lot. But you know, just being on the same team was enough to get touched by his personality. You'd hear him yelling and screaming, and you'd have to chuckle at the looks on their faces, the guys like Giff and Red [Webster] and Trip. But if one of the plays worked great in practice, especially a long pass, he'd never even stop to realize it was the defensive coach's problem. 'Hey, you, Tunnell,' he'd yell, 'who taught you how to cover a pass?' Well, you'd get a little scared of making a mistake, and if you didn't make any, he'd start yelling at his offensive players again. He kept us all on our toes."

One of Lombardi's favorite expressions of disapproval was: "You are really something, you are, mister." Tunnell heard it several times, but even more frequently from 1959, when he joined the Packers.

"I never knew what he really would be like when he got to be a head coach," Emlen says. "I knew him, of course, and I liked him, and he liked me, but Coach never took those things into account during a season. He treated us all as if we were trying to relax all the time, trying to get out of working hard. I'll say this: The first time I sat in on one of his pregame talks, I walked out of there with my palms sweating and my knees shaking. You were afraid to lose a game, because then you'd have to face him all over again. He was tough when we won."

Tunnell was one of those who wept openly at Lombardi's funeral.

Lombardi worked hard with the Giants, harder than many of the players had ever thought coaches worked. But he still found time to maintain his college loyalties, both with Fordham and West Point.

"He used to accompany me to every Fordham sports banquet," Wellington Mara remembers. "I haven't missed one in years, and neither did Vince. I think he was particularly touched when he was voted into the Fordham Hall of Fame, and honored at one of the annual banquets. Sentiment meant a lot to him, and tradition, and the past. He was an emotional man who tried hard all his life not to let those emotions show."

In 1958, Lombardi attended the Army-Navy game, and found it impossible to restrain himself. A friend remembers that Vince "kept jumping up and down, screaming at the Army players, yelling at Blaik, saying 'give the ball to Anderson, give it to Anderson.' When it was halftime, he started walking out, as if going to the locker. Then he caught himself, smiled a little embarrassed smile, and sat down again."

That year, Vince began thinking about being a head coach. "I remember that I worried about my age," he said later. "I was getting close to my middle forties, and I was still an assistant coach. It was much like when I was in my thirties and still a high-school coach. I got into coaching late, and I always felt I was behind all those young, bright guys who were coming into the field. I suppose I was impatient."

Mara remembers having seen signs of impatience the previous season. "Vince was offered a head coaching job in nineteen fifty-seven," he said, "which meant he would take over the team for the nineteen fifty-eight season. I don't think naming the team would serve any purpose. It wouldn't be fair to the club. But he came to me and asked for advice. I got as much information out of him as I could, made some telephone calls, and decided to advise him to stay in New York. The situation just didn't look right. There was a lot of age on the team in question, and it had had a poor season. I just didn't think there was much of a chance to rebuild it, and Vince could not stand for that much defeat. I told him he was doing a fine job with the Giants and that other teams were becoming aware of it, and that he would be hearing from others soon.

"He accepted what I had to say and decided to stay. I think it turned out well, all things considered."

What was in Lombardi's mind, of course, was coaching the Giants.

"When he came to me and told me about the offer from Green Bay," Mara recalls, "we sat down and looked at the situation there. The offer he had had the year before didn't shape up as much of a chance, but this one did. There was a good deal of talent on the Packers, young talent that could be developed. He had a chance to assume a position of authority, of command over his circumstances. It was the right job for him, and I advised him to take it.

"I could see one thing was still in his mind, the job in New York. I mean the head-coaching job. Jim Lee had told me he was tiring of it, but that he wanted to stay for another year or so, and I had to honor that request. I told Vince. I told him everything I knew about Jim Lee's status and about his considerations. I promised that I would offer the job to Vince when Jim Lee finally told me he didn't want it any longer, but I also told Vince that until such a time, I was morally committed to Howell. He understood perfectly, though I think he was a little bit regretful. He would have just loved to take over the Giants. It was his team and his town and his players."

Sid Gillman, whose departure from West Point in 1948 had opened the door for Lombardi there, also figured in Lombardi's move to Green Bay.

"Not too many people know," Gillman told Jerry Kramer, "but I helped Vinnie get the Green Bay job. I was attending an NFL draft meeting in nineteen fifty-eight—I was with the Rams by then—and as I came out of one of the meeting rooms, a few of the Green Bay people happened to be standing around. I knew one of the Green Bay directors, and he started telling me how hard they were searching for a new coach."

They wanted to replace Ray "Scooter" McLean, whose first and only season as head coach, 1958, had resulted in the Packers' worst record ever, 1–10–1. "Why don't you contact Vince Lombardi?" Gillman asked them. They did.

"I had seen Vince a lot during the middle nineteen fifties," Gillman said, "because whenever the Giants came to Los

Angeles he stayed at my place. We were very close friends. I knew Vince wanted to get out on his own. He'd never been a head coach anywhere except in high school. The fellow from Green Bay said he'd love to talk to Vince, and he got in touch with him almost immediately. That was it. He was hired."

Thus Lombardi's place as offensive coach of the New York Giants was vacated in the winter of 1958. The man named to replace him was Allie Sherman.

The Packers had been an incorporated, nonprofit organization since 1922—this status removed the team from receivership and kept it alive. In the late 1950's, as now, they were controlled by a board of directors, with sometimes as many as forty-five members. Dominick Olejniczak, a soft-spoken kindly man, is the president of the team, and he is the one who formally hired Lombardi.

The difference in style of the two men was soon apparent. Shortly after Vince had taken over the job, as general manager and head coach, Olejniczak phoned his office. "I'd like to come over and talk," he said.

"What about?" barked Lombardi.

"Oh, just about the team and the players. Just to chat."

"Make an appointment," Vince growled. "I'm too busy to just sit and talk. This team won only one game last year, and I don't have time to afford the luxury of sitting around and talking. I have work to do."

From then on. Lombardi was totally in command. "He ran the team," Ole admits, "and I took care of the business end of things. He didn't want any interference. Was I angry? No, I think not. Perhaps right at the beginning I was a little put off, but when I saw what a determined man we had, what a dedicated and intense person he was, I tried to understand. Winning was the only thing he thought about, and I certainly couldn't argue with the results. Now could I?"

Although Lombardi worked hard and long to transform the

Packers from jokes to winners, he kept in the back of his mind the thought of returning to New York as head coach. Just eleven months later, in 1960, Jim Lee Howell informed Well Mara that he wanted to be relieved of the head-coaching job after that season.

After informing Olejniczak of his intentions, Mara offered Lombardi the job. Lombardi said he would accept, if the Green Bay board of directors would allow him to terminate his contract, which still had some years to run. The Packers talked Vince out of leaving, pointing out that he had an obligation to remain and continue the job he had begun. Lombardi informed Mara that, with deep regrets, he had to turn down the job. He was going to stay in Green Bay.

"Sure, I was disappointed," Mara says. "I really would have loved to have Vince return as our coach. But I understood his reasons for declining, and I had to respect him for his decision. I knew how badly both he and Marie wanted to come home. He never did anything he felt was even slightly unethical, and if he could not get the Packers' approval, he could not just walk out on a contract. He was a man of his word."

Lombardi, too, was disappointed, and he seemed to bear some sort of indirect resentment toward Sherman, the Giants' eventual choice. They were to meet for the 1961 and 1962 NFL championships, as well as in several exhibition and regular-season games, and Lombardi's Packers always made it hot for Sherman's Giants. There was a noticeable coolness between these two men, who had worked together under Howell in 1957 and 1958, although neither would admit it.

"They respected each other," Mara recalls, "and Vince often remarked to me that the Giants under Sherman were the best-prepared athletes he ever had to compete against. But I guess he envied Allie's job, in a way. I'm sure he felt that way in the early nineteen sixties."

But in 1958, all Vince thought of was the opportunity that

had come to him in middle age, the chance to become a head coach in the NFL.

Perhaps not even Vince Lombardi realized the step he was about to take, and what he was to create in the frozen community of Green Bay, Wisconsin.

The Pride of
Green Bay

IT IS COLD IN GREEN BAY. THE SHRILL, ICY WIND STINGS; the snow comes early and stays late, piling layer upon layer through the winter; the temperatures drop below zero, nearly immobilizing the inhabitants.

In short, winter in Green Bay is foreboding. So, too, were Vince Lombardi's Packers. They were suited in manner and style to the unbearable weather conditions in which they played, for they were ruthless, relentless, and cruel in mastery.

Vince planned it that way. He brooked no interference, no letdown, no sign of weakness, no hint of rebellion. There simply was no time for it.

"I saw the movie *Patton*," said Frank Gifford, "and it was Vince Lombardi. The situation was different, but the thought was the same: We are here to do a job, and each and every one of us will put everything we have into getting that job done. That was Vince. Patton believed in reincarnation. Who knows? Maybe it was Patton who coached the Packers."

"I was thirty-six years old when I went to Green Bay," Emlen Tunnell recalls, "and I thought I had a little sophistication. But those pep talks of his. God! When I heard those pep talks, I'd cry and go out and try to kill people. Nobody else has ever been able to do that to me."

"Lombardi treats all of us the same," said the Green Bay defensive tackle Henry Jordan. "Like dogs."

"I guess I'm a typical product of Vince Lombardi," says guard Jerry Kramer. "I don't ever want to finish second at anything. I know that all I learned in football I learned from Vince Lombardi, and I'm going to be using it the rest of my life. 'Winning,' he would say, 'is not the most important thing. It's the only thing.' "

It was on January 28, 1959, that a forty-five-year-old former assistant coach named Vince Lombardi signed a five-year contract as general manager and head coach of the Green Bay Packers.

"This is the moment I have been waiting for all my life," Lombardi told a press conference. "I will put winning above all else here. Winning is gained through discipline. I've never been with a losing team before in my life, and I don't intend to start now."

This was, of course, an old song for the veteran reporters of the Green Bay-Milwaukee area. They had seen new men take over before, and they had heard the same promises and predictions. Some smiled. Others laughed aloud. But a few were in awe, and one of those few remembers today. He is Art Daley, sports editor of *The Green Bay Press-Gazette*.

"We didn't know very much about Vince aside from his record," Daley says. "He had built a creditable reputation as a competent assistant, a fine organizer, and a sound instructor. But really—and I don't think I'm being unfair—no one had any idea of what kind of a head coach he was going to make. He had never been one before, and it's a tall order to jump from assistant to boss and turn around a team that had been one, ten, and one. We didn't really believe all the things he said; we didn't disbelieve them, either. We simply felt he would change his tune when he saw the size of the job."

Once, in talking about the beginnings in Green Bay, Lombardi laid out the method of attack he used. "First, I watched all the films I could. Then I decided where our weaknesses were. I had two choices at that point—to fill in from our current material or to make trades. Fortunately, I was able to do both. We found some talent on the bench, and we got lucky with some waiver pickups and trades."

Sitting on the bench, having played little or not at all during the horrendous season of 1958, were the likes of Bart Starr, quarterback; Jim Taylor, fullback; the halfback-quarterback Paul Hornung; Jerry Kramer; Ron Kramer, tight end; Ray Nitschke, fullback; Bob Skoronski, tackle; and Fred "Fuzzy" Thurston, guard.

Juggling a bit, Lombardi switched Nitschke from fullback to middle linebacker and moved Hornung from quarterback to starting halfback, making him his place-kicker as well.

It started quickly for the original Packers of 1959. Going into summer training camp in July was like stepping into marine boot camp. One night, Lombardi wandered into the room where Jim Taylor and Jerry Kramer slept in the domitory at Saint Norbert's College. They were sitting on the edge of the bed, in socks and shorts.

"Jimmy," said the coach, "what time do you have?"

Taylor whipped out his watch and said, "It's eleven o'clock, sir."

"Jimmy," Lombardi responded, "you're supposed to be in bed at eleven, aren't you?"

"Yes, sir," said Taylor.

"That, Jimmy, will cost you twenty-five bucks," said Lombardi, and he strode back out into the corridor.

Taylor looked at Kramer and said: "Oh-oh. This guy's serious."

But Taylor had less trouble—far less, it might be said—with curfew and bedchecks than Hornung and McGee had. They were as intent on having fun as on becoming football stars.

It started quickly for those two.

At a team meeting one night, Lombardi found out that Max had sneaked out the night before. He revealed his knowledge before the entire squad and then started screaming at McGee. "Max, they say I'm tough. Well, I am. That'll cost you two hundred and fifty dollars. And if you do it again, it'll cost five hundred."

Shortly after, McGee made another clandestine foray, but this time he was caught speeding by the Wisconsin State Police. He promised them season tickets, passes to the locker rooms, anything, if only they would keep the time of night secret. They did not.

When Max got back to the dormitory, he could hear Lombardi walking up and down the halls, yelling: "Max, Max, where are you? Where are you, Max?"

The inevitable followed. "I warned you, Max," Lombardi choked. "I said that it would cost you five hundred, and it will. And if you go out again, it'll cost you a thousand." Then, according to eyewitnesses, Lombardi began shaking, realizing he was fighting a losing battle. Finally, he smiled. All those around him stared in disbelief. "Max," he said, "this might be tough, even for you, but if you can find something worth a thousand bucks to go sneaking out late for, call me and I'll go with you."

McGee, forever a blithe spirit, was the team pressure valve. Lombardi used him to dispel tension and strain, and Max never failed to come up with a gag line for just that purpose.

Once, later on in the Green Bay period, the Packers had lost a game in which they played badly. Lombardi was enraged. That Tuesday morning on the practice field he began to vent his irritation on the team.

"Gentlemen," he intoned, "I must be a terrible coach. I must have somehow failed you as a teacher and a leader. You forgot every basic fundamental about this game. We are going to have to start all over again, from scratch."

They waited, those proud Packers, for by now they were accustomed to their coach's tirades. Lombardi stopped, bent over, and picked up a football. Then, his voice dripping with sarcasm, he began anew.

"Gentlemen, the basics. First of all, this is a football."

From the back of the pack, McGee's high-pitched voice sang out: "Hang on a minute, Coach, you're going too fast."

It broke them up—Lombardi included—and the tension was gone. The Packers won their next game, 49–0.

Lombardi had taken over a down team, a team that had won only once in 1958. He determined that the fiber of the players was not tough enough, did not measure up to the standards he had set for himself and for those players he had worked with in New York. Toughening the Packers was his first chore.

"He yelled so long and so loud during his first week of summer camp," McGee remembered, "that he lost his voice." He made players who were injured run in practice. No one could interfere, and he took few suggestions. He was determined to sink or swim on his own results.

"You are preparing yourselves mentally," he told that first team. "It is tough now, but when the other team quits in the fourth quarter and you're still strong, you'll thank me. Don't cross me now. If it happens once, maybe it will go by. But if any one of you crosses me a second time, you're gone."

His first rehabilitation case was Hornung, an all-America quarterback at Notre Dame but an all-league disappointment since graduating and joining the NFL. Lombardi did not say he saw greatness in Hornung, but he did say that he needed a multiple-threat halfback such as Frank Gifford of the Giants. He appointed Hornung.

"You'll never be a quarterback," he told the man they came to call "Golden Boy." "You're just not good enough. But you can run, pass, kick, and block well enough. You're my half-back. The job is yours now, and the only way you can get out of it is to get yourself killed."

Hornung responded. He ran like the wind, blocked like a truck, threw the dangerous option passes, did all the place-kicking, and wound up leading the NFL in scoring, with ninety-four points.

The 1959 season started with a 9–6 victory over Green Bay's old rival, the Chicago Bears. Two more quickly followed, 28–10 over Detroit and 21–20 over San Francisco. Then the Los Angeles Rams humiliated Vince, 45–6. It was the worst defeat he was ever to suffer as a head coach.

But true to his word, Lombardi built a winner. The Packers finished the season with a 7–5 record. "About all we accomplished," the never-satisfied Lombardi commented, "was to win seven games and learn how it feels not to lose that many. We have much ahead of us."

"We should have won more games," he said, "but the people on this team just aren't accustomed to winning. They don't think like winners; they think they were lucky. That'll change. We have the makings here. I need some replacements, and I need to convince the rest of them that they are supposed to win. That's right, supposed to win."

For Vince Lombardi, the 1960 season began the day the 1959 season ended. He worked a fifty-two week schedule in Green Bay for as long as he was there, and could not under-stand coaches who took time off to "loaf and waste energy."

So in 1960, the Packers made it all the way to the top— almost. Their record, 8–4, was enough to win the Western Conference championship, with Detroit and San Francisco tied for second with 7–5. The Pack scored more points than any other team in the NFL that year, 332, and only San Francisco surrendered fewer, with 205, than the Packers' total of 209.

Lombardi had put it together at last, and the people of Green Bay knew they had a winner.

Hornung was incredible. He set a scoring record that still stands—176 points. He and Jim Taylor and Tom Moore took care of the running, and all cavorted to superb seasons. Starr was brilliant, as Starr always is. He didn't throw much, for the Packers played basic, ground-control football, but when he did, he was deadly. He completed 98 passes in 172 attempts for 1,358 yards. That's a fifty-seven percent record of completions, more than any quarterback—or coach—has a right to expect.

The blocking had just found the secret of Lombardi's coaching, and on those power slants and sweeps, Green Bay did not simply send a man out to block. The Packers sent a wave of men. "It was," recalled Sam Huff, then the New York Giants' middle linebacker, "a little like the guys who were in Korea told me about. You just couldn't get all the North Koreans because they kept coming. It was that way with the Packers."

So the Packers, because of their offense and a bone-crunching defense, were favored to defeat the Eastern Conference champion Philadelphia Eagles. Philadelphia, a 10–2 team, was sparked by the brilliant passing of Norm Van Brocklin, by the receiving of the little flanker Tommy McDonald, by the running of Ted Dean, and by the defense of Chuck Bednarik. The experts figured that a team that depended on the pass was not going to disturb the fundamental machine that Lombardi had assembled.

"We may not have a great team," Hornung said, "but we have a great coach. We'll play our hearts out for him, and if he asks us to play harder than that, we will."

Lombardi was impressed with the Philadelphia offense but more afraid of the defense. "Bednarik keys the whole team," he said. "I have never seen a middle linebacker with more mobility and range. When you must run to win, you hate to see a man like him on the other side. I'm looking for a close game, but we've got to stop Van Brocklin's passes. He's probably the best in the league, as a pure passer."

It turned into a brutal defensive affair. The Packers recovered the ball twice in the first quarter, once on a Bill Quinlan interception, again following a fumble. But Bednarik blunted the first drive on the Philly 5-yard line, and when the Packers ran into a fourth down on the second possession, Hornung kicked a 20-yard field goal.

"Right there," Lombardi was to say afterward, "was our downfall. When we got the ball twice in the first quarter and only got three points out of it, we lost. There was never a reason for it to be close after that first period, but we let them off the hook. We had them. It should have been fourteen to nothing. It is entirely our fault."

Others pointed to a missed Hornung field goal, with seconds remaining in the first half, from the Philadelphia 13. It meant that Philadelphia took a 10–6 lead into the locker room, instead of 10–9. The difference was to prove decisive.

Green Bay took the lead in the final quarter on a touchdown pass from Starr to Max McGee, after McGee, the punter, had run 35 yards on a fake kick. But the 13–10 lead should have been 16–10, and later, when the Eagles put across a touchdown, Green Bay should have trailed by only one point, not four.

If Hornung had made that short field goal in the first half, the strategy at the end would have been different, when the Packers penetrated deep into Eagles' territory. A field goal then could have won the game, 19–17. But Green Bay needed a touchdown. When the gun sounded, the Packers were on the Philadelphia 9-yard line, trailing 17–13.

"We were beaten by a better team," Lombardi told reporters.

"We should have won, and you know it," he told his players.

At the time, Lombardi felt that the loss was the biggest disappointment of his career. "You never know if you're going to get into a championship game," he said, "and when you do, you have to make the most of it. You can't afford a single mistake. Paul made several in this one, and the line missed some blocks, and the defense was not tough all the time. It was our fault, and we should have known better. I should have. I thought I had them ready, prepared. I'll just have to work harder."

To the players, most of them fairly pleased with coming so far in two seasons, this was no small source of fear. "How," Willie Davis, the all-pro defensive end, wondered, "can he make it any tougher? It's just not possible." Then Davis added, "But I know he will."

He did. The summer training camp of 1961 was, according to Davis, "as physically and emotionally draining as anything I've been through. I think Coach was afraid we'd play complacent football. He thought we were satisfied. My God, wouldn't he know we were more afraid of him than of any team?"

There are those who say the 1961 Packers were the finest team assembled in the history of the NFL. The club was compared to the 1941 Chicago Bears, the 1950 Cleveland Browns, the 1956 New York Giants. The record was 11–3, and the Packers scored 391 points in their fourteen games, far more than any other team in the league. For the third consecutive season, Hornung led the league in scoring, this time with 146 points. Taylor punched out more than 1,000 yards for the second straight year, his total of 1,307 finishing behind only the incomparable Jimmy Brown of Cleveland, who gained 1,408. But Taylor led the league in touchdowns, with 15.

Fully a dozen of the Packers made the all-pro team that season, an NFL record. They were Taylor, Hornung, Starr, Jerry Kramer, Ron Kramer, Forrest Gregg, Jim Ringo, Ray Nitschke, Willie Wood, Henry Jordan, Bill Forrester, and Willie Davis.

The starting lineups were enough to send small shivers of fear through the rest of the league. This was truly a machine, created in the image of its coach—tough, unrelenting, and merciless. "You can play this game only one way," Lombardi was fond of saying, "and that's all out, all the time. Anything less is inexcusable."

The offense consisted of Starr at quarterback, Hornung at halfback, Taylor at fullback, and Boyd Dowler at flanker. Ron Kramer was the tight end, Max McGee the split end. The tackles were Gregg and Bob Skoronski, the guards Jerry Kramer and Fuzzy Thurston, the center Ringo.

Defensively, the ends were Willie Davis and Bill Quinlan, the tackles Jordan and Dave Hanner. Nitschke was the middle linebacker, flanked by Dan Currie and Forrester. Hank Gremminger, Jesse Whittenton, Willie Wood, and Herb Adderley composed the secondary.

Green Bay swept to its conference championship, with an 8–5 Detroit team providing nominal opposition. But all the while, Lombardi kept tuned to the Eastern Conference race, where the Eagles, the Cleveland Browns, and the Giants battled through the entire season. It was not to be decided until the final game, when New York fought to a 7–7 tie against Cleveland. That gave the Giants a 10–3–1 record, to edge out Philadelphia, at 10–4. It had happened. Vince had the game he most wanted to play, matching the Pack with the Giants, a New York team that had most of Vince's former pupils in the starting lineups, a team coached by Allie Sherman, the man whose job Lombardi might have had.

"It was the greatest day of my life," he exulted later. "Just to play the Giants for the championship was more than I dared hope would happen."

The chartered United Airlines jet arrived in Green Bay Friday afternoon from New York, bringing with it the Giants, their coaches and owners, and a gaggle of newspaper reporters

—myself among them—who had covered the team all season. Most of us had never been to Green Bay, and we were totally unprepared for that hamlet of sixty thousand.

We had heard stories about Green Bay weather, but unless you are personally exposed to temperatures that drop to fifteen degrees below zero, such things remain only stories.

The sky was slate gray, and looking down just before our approach to the field, we city slickers saw the neat squares of farm land covered with snow. The sun seemed partially obscured by snowflakes, prompting Rosey Brown, the magnificent offensive tackle, to comment, "Look, the sun is wearing a coat, too."

Then we landed, and there was a crowd of natives at Stroebel Airport, curious to see what a team from New York looked like. The first man to step off the plane, the fullback Phil King, yelped back: "Stay there, guys. It's too cold to breathe."

The mercury was already at eleven below zero, and it was the middle of the afternoon.

The ride into town, where the team was to be quartered at the Northland Hotel, a relic of better days, was marked by the sight of thousands of stickers—on car bumpers and windows, on storefronts, on telephone poles, on childrens' schoolbooks. They said, simply, *Titletown, U.S.A.*

Sam Huff, gazing from his seat at a window, turned and yelled for the benefit of the busload, "Look, they spelled Tittle wrong." It was a typical Huff line, cocky and cynical. He was convinced the Giants were going to win the NFL championship. So were most of his teammates.

Allie Sherman, speaking years later, indicated that he was aware of the chances his Giants had in that game. "They were not very good," he admitted.

The Giants had acquired Y.A. Tittle at quarterback and the wide receiver Del Shofner in the summer of 1961, and the pair had combined to work miracles of offense not seen in

Yankee Stadium for many years. Tittle had been salvaged from a San Francisco team that had prematurely tabbed him as finished. The head coach there, Red Hickey, decided to utilize a "shotgun offense," in which the quarterback must do his share of running the ball. Tittle was, decidedly, not a runner. He was splayfooted and ran like a duck. He abhorred the thought of moving the ball on the ground. He was a classic passer, as intense a competitor as existed, a man totally convinced of his ability to win a game in the air.

Shofner, for him, was a revelation. He was a slightly built, lanky Texan, who had played for the Los Angeles Rams but had been out with injury during the greater part of the 1960 season. The Rams were thrilled to give him up for a number-one draft choice, and Delbert joined the Giants a week or so before Tittle.

They caught fire, as soon as Tittle wrested the starting quarterback job away from the old veteran Charlie Conerly, who nonetheless provided three or four crucial saves during the run to the Eastern championship.

It was a sound, solid offense. Tittle was a master at the screen pass, and Webster was his favorite beneficiary. No matter how many times he employed this dodge, he executed it so perfectly that it came as a shock to the defenders. Webster, with Phil King and Joel Wells, took care of the running. Gifford had received a serious concussion the season before from Chuck Bednarik, and was sitting out the season.

Joe Walton and Kyle Rote were the other receivers with Shofner, and the offensive line contained Rosey Brown, Jack Stroud, Ray Wietecha, and Darrell Dess—most of them former Lombardi pupils.

The defense was anchored by Huff in the middle, with Andy Robustelli at a defensive-end position. Indeed, the New York defensive line was the first to earn the "fearsome foursome" nickname now so commonly distributed.

With Robustelli were Dick Modzelewski and Rosey Grier

Vince Lombardi as one of Fordham's "seven blocks of granite."

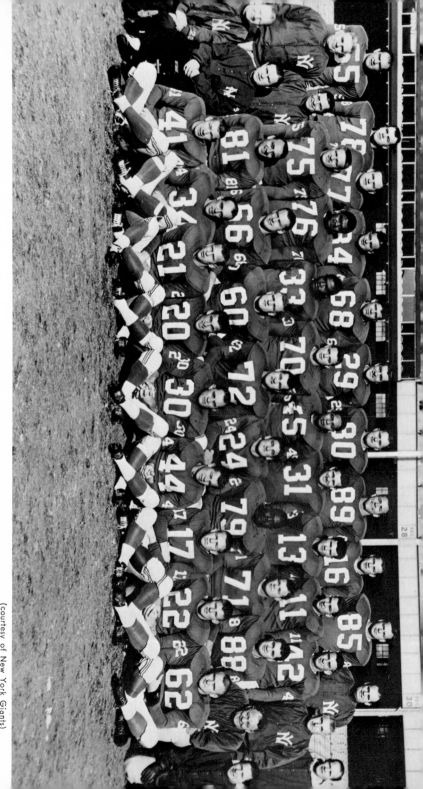

The New York Giants of 1958. Vince Lombardi, backfield coach, is second from left, third row up.

Lombardi of the Giants, with Jim Lee Howell. Below, he signs five-year contract with Packers. Dominick Olejniczak looks on.

Lombardi and staff. Hecker and Austin, left, Bengtson and Fears, right, all became head coaches.

(Vernon J. Biever Photo)

Disconsolate Lombardi walks off field after his only championship loss, to Philadelphia in 1960.

(Vernon J. Biever Photos)

How sweet it was: Ron Kramer carrying Patton and Huff across goal line in '61 win over Giants.

The famous Green Bay sweep. Jim Taylor (31) is the ball carrier. "Fuzzy" Thurston (63) blocks.

Four who made the Green Bay Packers great: Paul Hornung and Bart Starr (top), Jim Taylor and Willie Davis (below).

at the tackles—"Ro and Mo" as the team called them—and Jim Katcavage at the other end. Huff was flanked by Cliff Livingston and Tom Scott. The secondary consisted of Dick Lynch and Erich Barnes on the corners, and at safeties Jimmy Patton and Joe Morrison, who was filling in for the injured Al Webb.

Morrison had a particularly rough time. He was assigned to —or in the vicinity of—the hulking Ron Kramer, Green Bay's 6 foot 3 inch, 240-pound tight end. Joe was to take over the flanker spot from Rote in the years ahead, and he became an extraordinary offensive player. But he was not yet ready for the sort of defensive workout the Packers gave him that day.

Before the game, Lombardi had expressed concern, not so much for the Giants as for the condition of the field. It was buried under a heavy tarpaulin, a foot of hay and fourteen inches of new snow. "If the field is in good condition, so are we," he said. "If the ground isn't frozen, our blockers will be able to get their footholds. Taylor and Hornung will be able to cut, and our receivers can make all the fakes and execute all the tricky moves to get clear.

"If all these things happen, we'll win."

This was the first championship game I had ever covered, and a yellowed duplicate of the story I sent to my newspaper the day before the game shows the impact Lombardi had on the town.

"Vince Lombardi is the exalted leader of this pint-sized Wisconsin ice cube," it said. "Whatever Vince Lombardi says is true—unquestionably. His followers, the entire hysterical population of 60,000, believe every sagacious syllable. Green Bay is laboring under the premature assumption that the Packers are already the champs. After all, Lombardi promised it to them, didn't he?"

It was the first championship played at Green Bay, although the Packers had been involved in five previous games. And the residents, proud of being the smallest town in the NFL, were delirious with Coach Lombardi's vows of victory.

The only serious injury sustained by the Packers during the season was a fractured ankle suffered by Jerry Kramer, the all-league guard. Lombardi, however, a master at improvising, moved his all-league tackle, Forrest Gregg, to the guard spot and filled Gregg's position with young Norm Masters, who played remarkably well.

"When Jerry got hurt," Masters recounted, "and Coach moved Gregg, I was told I had to play tackle. Coach told me I just had to, because there was no one else. But he said I would be forgiven no mistakes, because I was being paid to play football, and now I was coming off the bench to do what I was supposed to do. He told me the fortunes of the entire team rested on the performance I gave. I was so afraid of failing Coach that I know I played far better than I ever did before. He made a man feel important."

Lombardi had been handed a setback in midseason, when three of his stars—Hornung, Dowler, and Nitschke—were called up by the National Guard and sent to Fort Lewis, Washington. "We hit our peak against the Cleveland Browns on October fifteenth," he said. "We beat them forty-nine to seventeen, and at that moment I felt we had the greatest football team ever assembled. Then our soldiers had to leave, and we lost that razor-sharp edge."

As one pundit put it: "Lombardi did not begrudge the army those three men, but he would have preferred to see the Russians invade Milwaukee before he gave them up."

They were all able to get weekend passes, however, and they, too, were ready for the Giants. The date was December 31, 1961, the latest date for a championship game to that time.

By eleven o'clock that morning, the Packers had arrived at the locker room of City Stadium—since enlarged and renamed Lambeau Field. As each man entered, he passed under a huge sign Lombardi had pinned up over the doorway. It read:

What You See Here,
What You Say Here,
What You Hear Here
. . . Let It Stay Here
When You Leave Here

One hour before the game, Lombardi toured the field, supervised the removal of the tarp, and found the ground "in July condition."

"Under all that cover," one of the men told me, "the grass had actually been growing."

Lombardi decided the Packers would wear cleats, not sneakers, as the field was not frozen and the temperature had soared to fifteen degrees above zero. He then went back to the locker room, to deliver his pregame pep talk.

"I know you can win," he told the players. "So let's not make any mistakes. You know you should have won the championship last year. This game means a lot to all of you, and to me. To you it means money and prestige. To me, because it's the Giants, it means much personal satisfaction. Be alert. Avoid fear. Let's get 'em."

Then, as had become customary, Lombardi and the assistant coaches left for the field, while Starr and Jim Ringo conducted a quick team meeting. The Pack ran out onto the field. So, too, did the Giants, but they needn't have bothered.

The first time Green Bay got the ball, on a punt after Rote had dropped a sure touchdown pass out in the open, the pattern of the day began to unfold. Hornung ran for 2. Then Hornung ran for 6. Then Hornung ran for 1. The Packers had to punt—for the first and last time of the game.

Again Tittle found Rote in the clear, and again Rote dropped a long bomb. Again the Giants punted, and now the game turned for good in favor of the Packers.

Hornung ran for 4, gained 26 on a pass from Starr, then

ran for 5. Taylor, hampered by a sore back, gained 13 on three consecutive carries. Then Hornung broke loose for 7 more and a first down on the Giants' 25.

As the first quarter ended three plays later, the Packers were on the New York 6. From there, Hornung took a handoff from Starr and cracked through right tackle. He scored, and kicked the extra point.

He added a field goal of 17 yards shortly after, and by the time the half had ended, Starr had thrown twice for touchdowns, to Ron Kramer and Max McGee. The halftime totals showed Hornung with 12 points, the rest of the Packers with 12 more, and the Giants with aching bruises.

In the second half, Paul added two more field goals and an extra point. The Packers scored again cn another Starr-to-Kramer pass, in which the bullish Kramer dragged Huff and Patton into the end zone with him, standing up. The final score of the game was 37–0, and the Giants had settled for survival, which was no small accomplishment.

Hornung had established a still-standing NFL championship game scoring record of 19 points. The Giants had been held to one first down rushing and four by passing. Green Bay had piled up nineteen first downs and 345 yards gained, to 130 for New York. Tittle, and then Conerly, had completed ten of twenty-nine passes, while Starr hit on ten of nineteen for 164 yards and three touchdowns. The Packers, exulting in ball control, ran off sixty-three plays from scrimmage to the Giants' forty-three, and gained an average of 4.1 yards a play—to New York's 2.2.

It was a crushing, humiliating defeat, and the Giants were still in shock sitting on the bus waiting for the trip home.

Greg Larson, then a rookie tackle who later became an all-pro center, remembered crying with the shame of it. And the pain. "When we got behind like that," he said, "the Green Bay defensive line dared us to run. They knew we had to pass to catch up. They came in swinging from the heels, with fists and forearms and elbows. It was the most awesome thing I've ever been involved in. We had no way to stop them. They were like wild men. It was unending, it seemed. They constantly punished us."

For Vince Lombardi, this New Year's Eve celebrated his greatest victory. "You people are the greatest team in the history of the league," he told his players.

There was no one to argue. "We won all the big ones all year, and this was the biggest of them all," he told reporters. "It was a determined effort by a dedicated team. Hornung was superb, but so were all the rest. He needed the blocks, remember, and Starr needed the protection, and we needed the defensive fury that kept the Giants at bay. It all worked right. We achieved a plane I don't think any team has ever achieved. I am very proud of this team."

He was kind in victory. "I hope you people don't think the Giants are thirty-seven points worse than we are," he cautioned. "For all we know, they can play us again for the championship next year and win by the same score. It got out of hand for them, that's all. You'll find that the biggest scores in crucial games are usually when two teams of equal ability have played. They had to change their game when we got ahead."

Lombardi was prophetic. The teams did meet again the following season, in Yankee Stadium.

Neither team had any difficulty in repeating as conference champion. The Packers were 13–1 and the Giants 12–2. The only surprise was that New York clinched first, with a victory in Chicago. The Packers, hotly pursued by the Detroit Lions, who finished 11–3, locked it up a week later. Green Bay was awesome in taking its third consecutive conference title, scoring 415 points while giving up just 148. Both figures were the best in the league. The Giants, again strong on offense, had scored 398, second to Green Bay. But they had allowed 283, which was only fourth best.

This time Taylor, with nineteen touchdowns, won the league scoring title. He finally gained more ground than Cleveland's Jimmy Brown and led the league on rushing with 1,474 yards. Starr was the league's passing champion, and Willie Wood was the leader in interceptions.

Vince himself always felt this team was his finest. From the start of summer camp, he drilled one thought into the players: "Once you're on top, everybody wants to knock you off. This is the real test. This year you find out whether or not you're really champions."

Hornung, who had been discharged from the army, reported to camp out of condition. "Paul, you look like you're carrying a piano on your back," Lombardi told him. "I'll either work you back into shape, or you'll be so tired you'll stay home at night." Hornung responded, and opened the season as the starting halfback, scoring three touchdowns, two field goals, and four conversions for 28 points. But the next week he tore knee ligaments, and Tom Moore finished out the season for him.

Starr had accomplished Lombardi's goals. He became the complete quarterback, methodical and poised under any circumstance. He completed sixty-two percent of his passes, still an NFL record.

The Giants, again behind Tittle and Shofner, had run away with the Eastern Conference race. They clinched easily and early, and several of the players said the season would be a total waste if the Packers did not win in their conference. The proud Giants, still smarting from their ignominy, wanted revenge.

It came to pass. The date was December 30, 1962.

Lombardi returned to New York as a member of the enemy. "I love this town," he said. "I like it in Green Bay, and I'm content to remain there, but I love New York. You can't get a thing like that out of your system."

Lombardi had come in on a Wednesday, and journeyed to

northern New Jersey to visit his parents. He spent time in New York City, seeing sportswriters and a legion of former friends. But the game was uppermost in his thoughts. "It's New York," he said, "and I know how New York fans can help the Giants. And the Giants won't need any help to get ready for us. They still remember the score last year."

They remembered. For the two weeks before the title game, there was a sign hanging prominently in the New York dressing room. It had no words, just a number—*37*. The numerals were two feet high.

"That game," said Robustelli before the rematch, "was the low point of my career. We have done a great deal with defense for the Giants, and that one really stings. It burned into my brain, and the only way I can get rid of the memory is by returning the aggravation. If we win this game, it won't be enough. We have to destroy the Packers and Lombardi. It's the only way we can atone for what happened to us last year."

Robustelli was deadly serious. So, too, was Tom Scott, one of the finest and meanest linebackers the Giants have ever had. He would get himself up for a game by punching the lockers and walls before going out on the field. He had been accused of being a dirty player, but he always denied it. "Sometimes the game gets into me," he said, "and I take it all personally. I hate people trying to gain yardage. I try to hit them as hard as I can, and as often as I can. But I never intend to hurt a man. I think other players can understand that." Jimmy Brown was one who never could. He accused Scott of trying to "put out my eyes" in one crucial game in 1963.

Despite the one-sidedness of the 1961 game, most observers felt the Giants would have the edge. They were on their home field, and Tittle had been marvelous all season. And the weather just couldn't be as bad as it had been in Green Bay a year before. It was. It was worse.

The winds howled at gale force, and the cold tore around the field in fury. Yankee Stadium, constructed in 1923, is a haven for violent air currents, and the old place was at its foreboding worst. "Never have I seen a worse day for football," Lombardi remarked to one of his aides when they arrived at the stadium in the late morning. "I'm half-sorry to ask people to play in these conditions."

But play they did, and it was a game marked by a rare ferocity. Hornung was pronounced fit and started, but he was not the same Paul who had phantomed past the Giants in 1961. Therefore, the brunt of the offense fell to Jim Taylor, once Starr—and Tittle, as well—found passing impossible.

"I'd put the ball in the air," Starr said, "and it would start blowing back to me. I never experienced that before. I knew right away I would have to use more running plays, and as great a passer as Y.A. was, I felt he would be under the same handicap as I was. It was not a day for passing the ball, not hardly."

Taylor, then, was it. No one ever played tougher football, and no one ever earned Lombardi's respect more than his 6 foot, 215-pound graduate of Louisiana State University. Time after time, Taylor hurled himself at the Giants' defense, called the finest in the league, and time after time, they threw him back.

"The ground was like concrete," Taylor remembered, "and the Giants were even tougher. It was this game that showed me the value of working under Coach Lombardi all those years before. I think he knew something like this was going to come to us, and he had us prepared for it. I don't think I could have played as hard as I did without the seasoning he gave us. He taught us to be tough. He taught us to withstand pain, and he taught us that if we can hold out, the other team will crack first. It was the Coach who ran for me in that game. I just kept hearing him yelling and pushing us to more and more."

It was guerilla warfare, and the Packers were the equal of the Giants. Taylor was the difference, combining determination with a vicious pride. Robustelli, Huff, Modzelewski, and Grier battered him unmercifully. He kept coming back. Modzelewski charged later that Taylor had bitten him, and Taylor accused Huff of trying to "cripple me with knees and elbows." Many grudges were born on that frozen field, and they are still alive today.

Hornung, because of his knee injury, was no longer the place-kicker. Jerry Kramer was. He kicked a 26-yard field goal in the first quarter to put the Packers on the scoreboard. Green Bay made it 10–0 in the second quarter, following a fumble by Phil King that Nitschke recovered on the New York 28. Hornung, sweeping to his right, suddenly cocked his arm and passed for 20 yards to Boyd Dowler on the Giants' 8. Then Taylor burst up the middle over Grier and Huff for the touchdown.

But the Giants fought back. With McGee standing in the Green Bay end zone to punt, Erich Barnes broke through and blocked the kick. Jim Collier, a reserve end, fell on the ball, scoring a touchdown for the Giants. It was 10–7. Now, on fourth and 2, Kramer kicked a 29-yarder. It was 13–7. But a New York touchdown could still win.

It was the fourth quarter. Neither side was giving any more. Finally, Green Bay accepted a Don Chandler punt on its 28 and began to move—with difficulty, with pain, with fatigue—but move they did.

Taylor punched out 6 and Moore 3. Taylor made 5 for the first down, then 2 more to the Green Bay 45. Hornung escaped for 8 to the New York 47, and Taylor ripped off another 6 to the 41. Now came one of the crucial plays, with Hornung on the bench. Moore, taking a handoff to his left, slipped past one tackler and streaked to the New York 28, a gain of 13 vital yards.

But further plays resulted in a net gain of only 5 yards. With 1:56 remaining in the game, Kramer was called in to kick from the 30. It was pressure football. His kick was good. The score: Green Bay 16, New York 7.

Now the Giants rallied. Starting from their 26, they began to battle the Packers and the clock. Tittle, on third down, hit Shofner for 19 to the New York 45. There was 1:08 to play. Tittle found Webster with a short pass to the 50, then was incomplete to Shofner. And then with 40 seconds left, Green Bay was called for offsides, giving the Giants a first down on the Packers' 45.

With Lombardi raging and fuming on the sidelines, the Giants began to pick up momentum, as if the error from the usually impenetrable Packers had given them heart. Tittle threw to Walton for 13 yards, down to the Green Bay 32, and the Giants took their final time out with 33 seconds to play. It was now, with time for perhaps three more passes, that the Packers felt a stab of fear. Now, with a second world's title within Green Bay's grasp, the Giants had turned it around.

Tittle's throw to Walton down the right sideline was just barely incomplete. Now 20 seconds remained—the longest 20 seconds Lombardi said he had ever known.

The play was called Circle-34. It it a fullback pass play. The fullback was Alex Webster, who ran a circle pattern out of the backfield, broke across the middle of the field, and got to the end zone.

"My God, he's free," Lombardi screamed as the play unfolded. "He's there. They're going to do it. My God, where is the coverage?"

Webster was there, and Tittle saw him. The wind was with Tittle. The ball was well thrown, but it was nudged off course, and Alex went to his knees in a frantic attempt to gather in the pass. It slipped just pass his fingertips.

With 8 seconds remaining, a pass to Walton was good to the Green Bay 7-yard line. Tittle was often to speak of "one more play," but the clock denied him.

What would he have done from the 7? "I'd have run it in, a reverse, right down the left sideline. Nobody would have expected that, not even Lombardi."

The Pack had won, 16–7, and they had their second championship in two years.

After the game, Lombardi credited Hornung with the big play in the drive to the field goal that put the Giants more than a field goal away. The Packers were on their 45 with a third-and-6 situation. Starr called on his Golden Boy one more time.

Paul moved to his right with the ball, brought up his arm as if to pass once again, then tucked it away and lowered his head. He ran into Robustelli, and drove both Andy and Modzelewski back. He made 7 yards when 6 were needed, 7 of the toughest yards he had ever been asked to produce.

"It was right in front of our bench," Lombardi glowed afterward. "It seemed to arouse all of us. Paul has a way of doing that. The guys on the bench started to yell and scream, and the team knew that if Hornung—sore shoulder and sore knee and all—could do that, they could stop the Giants. The bigger the game, the bigger the play Paul Hornung comes up with. It was the key to the game for us. The team had been quiet before that, I guess because of the cold. But that play brought everyone to their feet. The defense caught fire. We knew we had them."

Then he turned to the matter of the game. "It was one of the toughest games I've ever seen. I'm very proud of them. They played a great game."

Nitschke, with one interception and two fumble recoveries, was named the game's most valuable player and was awarded a sports car. Asked what he was thinking about during the game, Ray responded: "We just thought about winning. We never even thought about losing. Why should we? We have Vince Lombardi, don't we?"

The next day, Lombardi sat down with a reporter and talked more about the game. "I didn't say much of anything to the players after that one," he began. "We just said a little prayer of thanksgiving. Defensively, we were superb. Over-all, we played a better game today than we had played for the second half of the season. I'm not interested in statistics, just in the final score. All I know is we won, and that's enough for me.

"I think it was as fine a football game as I've ever seen. I think we saw football as it should be played. We saw great tackling, fine blocking, and great pursuit—and I'm talking about both teams."

Later on, during a rare and brief resting period, Lombardi talked about the league and Green Bay's position in it since his arrival: "When they point out that there are two divisions in the NFL, they are so right. Any pro football man not sticking up for his own group will tell you that the West is considerably tougher than the East. It is in the West that we must survive against such as Detroit and Chicago, just to name two. You have to be strong to do that, and you must remember that we have reached a status comparable to that of the New York Yankees in baseball. Teams we figure to beat rather handily play like maniacs against us. All our opponents keep getting harder to handle in an all-out effort to knock off the champs.

"It's difficult to keep even a pro team emotionally high week after week. But I have a lot of faith in our guys. They have a lot of pride. We are a young team, but some of the older hands will be replaced. Hornung was the key to our game. There are players who hit harder straight ahead, run outside better, pass on the option as well, and place-kick as accurately and as far. But no one I ever saw did all these things as effectively as Paul. His knee will be all right, too. All he has is a bad cartilage strain, which healed perfectly and requires only two months of complete rest."

Then Lombardi looked at the prospects for 1963, and smiled. "We'll have to get tougher," he said. "We'll have to be even better."

Not even Lombardi could foresee the betting scandal that would rock the sports world during the off season and the loss of Paul Hornung.

The Pack Comes Back

ON APRIL 17, 1963, FOLLOWING MONTHS OF INVESTIGA-tion, the office of Pete Rozelle, National Football League Commissioner, released the following bulletin:

"The Commissioner has suspended indefinitely Paul Hornung, Green Bay halfback, and Alex Karras, Detroit tackle, for placing bets on their own teams and on other NFL games . . ."

Green Bay was in shock. The residents of the town, accustomed to the sight of Hornung wearing number five on his jersey, could not believe he was lost for at least the coming season. But it was so, and Rozelle made it particularly clear that if the two players were to be reinstated at all it would not be soon. "Yes," he answered a questioner, "that precludes the 1963 season."

Art Daley of *The Green Bay Press-Gazette* remembers the day. "People walked around on the streets, and they had this sort of numbed look on their faces. Their words were all about

Paul, and it generally took on all the appearance of a town in mourning. Here he was, the most famous football player in the world, the Golden Boy, and he belonged to a little town like ours. They were confused and hurt, almost personally hurt."

Lombardi was crushed. He had come to think of Paul almost as a son.

"I asked him straight out if he had done those things," Lombardi said, "and he admitted he had. But he repeated that he had never bet against the Packers. He was as dejected as I have ever seen any man, but he was guilty, and he had to pay the penalty. I was disappointed in him, and of course I was worried about the rest of the team."

Hornung's loss could not have come at a worse time than the 1963 season. The Packers, still awesome themselves, discovered that they were locked in a struggle with the tough Chicago Bears, whose defense had become almost impenetrable under an assistant coach named George Allen.

These two teams were scheduled to face each other twice— once on opening day, once near the end of the season.

Green Bay was beaten in that first game, 10–3, the only time in a season of fourteen games that the Packers would be held without a touchdown. Chicago won the second match, as well, 26–7. These were the only two losses for the Packers in 1963. Chicago took the Western Conference championship and then capped the season with a 14–10 victory over the Giants for the NFL championship. New York won its Eastern Conference title handily, scoring a near-record 448 points, allowing just 280, and sending eight players to the Pro Bowl.

"It's a rather strange feeling," Allie Sherman said before the Bears' game. "Of course, I am delighted that we won our third conference title, and I am most pleased with the efforts of the team. But I am a bit disturbed that the Packers did not win with us. I was hoping for another crack at Mister Lombardi."

The Packers finished the season with an 11–2–1 record—

there had been a 13–13 tie with Detroit. Their record was better than the Giants' 11–3, but they could get no closer to the championship game than the seats at Wrigley Field in Chicago.

Near the end of the 1963 season Lombardi disclosed, in an interview with Dave Brady of *The Washington Post,* that President Kennedy had "suggested" that Vince take the position of head coach at West Point. Dale Hall, who followed Earl Blaik, had been dismissed after the 1961 season, and the job was open. West Point officials went all out, knowing how much the Lombardis missed living in the East.

"Oh, I think the President must have been joking," Lombardi said. "He was laughing when he made the remark. It was before anyone else had been considered for the job. As I remember, the President said to me: 'Vince, can't we do something about getting you to take that coaching job up at Army?'

"I just laughed, and the President did not press the point. But he wanted to talk more football. He knows what's what."

Lombardi must have given it serious thought. He had always loved the West Point life, and there was the temptation to go back East. But West Point could not match Green Bay in salary. And for Lombardi, there was also something else. "The game is the same," he once said, "but there's a world of difference in the ability of the players. When they get to the pros, you know two things about them. First, they are the cream of the crop. Second, they want to play football very badly. College boys sometimes use football as a means of attaining an education, which is fine, but that fire isn't there to compete and be the best."

If the rewards of pro football were greater, so too could the disappointments be. Lombardi had wanted that fourth consecutive championship badly. Those two games against the Chicago defense had blocked the way. Elsewhere, Green Bay appeared to be as mighty as ever. There was, for instance, a game in Saint Louis that the Pack won 30–7, beating a team that had gained 1,045 yards in the previous two weeks. The Cardinals completed only eight passes in the first half and fell behind, 21–0. The rest of the afternoon was a lesson in frustration for the Saint Louis quarterback, Charley Johnson.

"It seemed," he said later, "that when we had the ball, Green Bay had more than eleven men on the field."

Yet even in victory, the Pack seemed less confident— lethargic, some said—without Hornung. "We were looking for the big play that he always came up with to getting us going," said Boyd Dowler, "but he wasn't there, and we all sensed his absence. It's difficult to lose your threat that way and not feel it."

"I'm tired," said Jim Taylor. The big fullback gained more than 1,000 yards for the fourth consecutive season, but he was carrying more of the offensive burden without Hornung beside him in the backfield. "I'm just not in shape."

Hornung's replacements—Tom Moore, Elijah Pitts, and Earl Gros—did well, but the rhythm and cohesiveness of offense that Lombardi had labored to build were not there. The Packers were by no means floundering. They were also not what they had been in 1962, and Chicago was the gainer.

Almost like a person who has suffered a personal loss and becomes more accident-prone, the Packers began to have injuries. The worst was Bart Starr's fractured passing hand, which made team morale sink farther. "We can still come up for the big games, and I think we have the necessary talent," Lombardi said, "but if we don't stay whole we don't have a chance."

Lombardi also acknowledged that some of his players were aging. He told reporters that his chief problem for the coming season would be bringing in some replacements. "I can't afford to have the young players learn while they play," he said. "You lose games that way. Perhaps it's not fair of me, but I want them to learn from practices and scrimmages and from watching the games on the bench. I want them ready when they get called."

The slowing down of the Packers was no more evident than in the second game with the Bears. The conference title was at stake. Green Bay went in with haughty arrogance. The Packers were, after all, the champions, and they had won the big games when they had to. Lombardi did not think this one would be any different, although he was the first to praise the Bears' defense.

"No defense, not ours, not New York's, not Cleveland's, not Detroit's . . . is any better than Chicago's. Coach Halas has done a remarkable job. But if anyone feels the Bears' *offense* is weak, he is mistaken. This is a fine, balanced, competent team."

The game was a horror for the Packers. Seven times Green Bay turned over the ball—twice on fumbles, five times on interceptions. Lombardi, the ball-control wizard, watched Chicago beat him at his own game, as the Bears ran seventy-four plays to Green Bay's fifty-two. The ever-changing Chicago defense kept the Packers off balance. Chicago did not seem to show the same defensive alignment twice. More than anything else, this upset the rigid blocking patterns of the Packers' offensive line. It was chaos, and Lombardi was the first to admit it.

"They beat both our lines, and they guessed at what we were going to do before we knew what we had in mind," he said. "We have no right to think we could have won this game."

And so the Packers were dethroned.

By the following season, it was the Bears' turn to feel the effects of age and injury. The Packers had now retooled, had brought in some fresh, young athletes. They were coming on again, determined to reverse the results of 1963.

But now there was a new threat to contend with—the indomitable Baltimore Colts, paced by the finest practitioner of quarterbacking in the world, Johnny Unitas. The schedule-makers pitted the Packers against Chicago and then against the Colts in the first two games of the 1964 season.

Green Bay salvaged some satisfaction by beating the Bears in the opener, 23–12, and that was the kind of season it was going to be for the Bears. But now, primed and ready, Green Bay lost a home-field decision to Baltimore, 21–20. The Colts were buoyed by this victory over a team most football people still considered great. It was to prove a fateful success. "When we saw we were able to beat Green Bay," Unitas recalled, "we felt we really did have a shot at the whole thing."

For the second year in a row, the Packers would lose twice to the team that won the conference championship. The margin of defeat came to a total of four points—21–20 and 24–21. Lombardi restlessly began to experiment with the starting positions. Injuries hurt him—to Starr, to Gregg, to other key players.

But there were two signs of hope for the Packers. Paul Hornung had returned, having been pardoned by Commissioner Rozelle on March 16, after a full review of the case. Secondly, the younger men began making their presence felt. There were Lionel Aldridge, the defensive end who took over for Bill Quinlan; Ron Kostelnik, at defensive tackle for Dave Hanner; two new linebackers, Dave Robinson and Lee Roy Caffey, who replaced Bill Forrester and Dan Currie; and three new defensive backs, Bob Jeter, Herb Adderley, and Doug Hart, replacing Hank Gremminger, Jesse Whittenton, and John Symank.

Offensively, the new Packers included Carroll Dale, a fleet wide receiver traded by Los Angeles who relegated McGee to the bench (although Max still had a chapter of glory to come); Ken Bowman at center, succeeding Jim Ringo who had gone to the Eagles in the trade for Caffey; and Bill Anderson, an experienced and gifted tight end acquired from Washington to fill Ron Kramer's position.

Baltimore won the 1964 Western Conference championship with a splendid 12–2 record, while the Packers had slumped to 8–5 by the end. The fact that the Colts were ambushed by the Eastern champion, Cleveland, in the title game, 27–0, did not dim the sheen of Baltimore's accomplishment, nor would it make the chore of unseating Don Shula's team in 1965 any less difficult.

But the Packers would start the new season with Hornung back in form. Despite his presence on the team during the 1964 season, the year away had cut into his conditioning and timing. He had been far from sharp and needed a season to regain his footing.

He was ready in 1965, as were the rest of the Packers. It was a particularly intense winter of preparation for Lombardi. He once said he knew more about the shape of his 1965 team, and earlier, than of any of his teams before or after.

"We have a big job to do," he said, "and we are going to do it. Two years in a row is too long for us to have been left out of championship games. We will win it this season."

Don Chandler, who had spent a successful career as a punter and place-kicker with the Giants, was acquired by the Packers. Chandler, a dour Oklahoman, had asked the Giants for permission to work out with the team only on weekends, so that he might pursue his real-estate business in Tulsa. Sherman and Wellington Mara refused, and he asked to be traded.

"A player like that, once he gets to be unhappy, really should be traded," Sherman had said. "He will carry the resentment all season, and it could affect everyone."

So Chandler went to the Packers, and he had a long, long talk with Vince. "I thought I had heard all the coaching speeches," he said. "I was convinced of what I wanted to do, and I told him that when we first sat down. An hour or so later, I couldn't wait to change my plans. I'll say this about Vince Lombardi: He was hypnotic when he wanted to be. I remember the first time I sat in when he delivered one of those pregame speeches. When it was over, I was afraid to miss a field goal, not because we might lose, but because I'd have to face him afterward."

The Pittsburgh Steelers opened the 1965 season for Green Bay, and the Packers won, 41–9. A crucial game with the Colts ended in a 20–17 Green Bay victory, followed by decisions of 23–14 over the Bears, 27–10 over San Francisco, 31–21 over the Lions, and 13–3 against Dallas. Undefeated in six games, the Pack was sprinting toward a conference championship.

Then, for the second time in his Green Bay career, Lombardi watched the Packers lose two straight, 31–10 to Chicago, 12–7 to Detroit. What had been a runaway suddenly turned into a tight race. The Colts had been granted a reprieve, and they made the most of it.

The Packers stopped their skid with a hard 6–3 victory over Los Angeles, and followed up with a 38–13 decision over the Vikings. Then a visit to California resulted in a 21–10 defeat. Now the Packers were 8–3. The Colts were right behind them. A Packer victory the next week, 24–19 over the Vikings, made it 9–3. The Colts were next.

The game was in Baltimore, on December 12, 1965. It is a date no Packer fan will ever forget. Neither, for that matter, will any Colts' fan.

Hornung was not well. He had suffered a pinched nerve in his neck, which at times made his right arm useless. He had hurt his legs again, and his back was bruised. He had spent much of the previous two games on the bench, allowing Pitts and Moore or the rookie Junior Coffey to spell him.

But this was for the money, and Hornung was a money player.

Lombardi took the Packers to a motel outside Washington five days before the game. "I wanted them to have full privacy, to have no distractions, to have nothing else to do but think about the game with Baltimore. It was the most important game we had had to play in three seasons, and nothing was going to hurt our chances if it could be prevented. I even moved the curfew up to ten thirty instead of eleven. We had to win."

Privately, Lombardi was most concerned about Hornung. He asked Paul if he thought he could play, and the handsome, blond superstar, shrugging off his injuries, assured the coach he could. "Don't worry about the Colts, Coach," Hornung said. "It's in the bag."

Baltimore, too, had had injuries. The most serious was to Unitas, who had torn knee ligaments two games before and was in a cast. Unitas's replacement, Gary Cuozzo, would be starting only his second pro game. But his first, against Minnesota, had been exhilarating for the young man signed as a free agent out of Virginia University. He had thrown five touchdown passes.

The day was foggy and misty. It seemed made for a memorable game.

Hornung made it so. He steeled himself for what had to be done, and then outdid even himself. He was a ghost returned from 1961 and 1962, flitting here and there, throwing passes, catching passes, blocking furiously. He scored five touchdowns, gained 61 yards in fifteen carries and caught two passes. His blocking opened holes for Taylor that the line hadn't gotten to, and big Jim added 66 snarling, smashing, up-the-middle yards.

The final score was 42–27.

"I got my legs back for the first time this season," Hornung said later in the Green Bay dressing room. "I guess all that rest here did it, huh?"

Hornung—and Lombardi—were quick to point out a defensive play near the end of the first half that, they felt, had turned the game into victory. Green Bay held a 14–13 lead, after Paul's first two touchdowns. Then Baltimore recovered a fumble on the Packers' 2-yard line. A Baltimore lead at halftime seemed certain.

Cuozzo called a play-action pass. The halfback, Lenny Moore, would fake a carry up the middle, and Jerry Hill, the fullback, would slip to the outside and turn down into the end zone for a short, looping pass. But Willie Davis and Dave Robinson diagnosed the play. Davis leaped and deflected Couzzo's pass—right into Robinson's arms. Robinson caught it and then, turning on all the speed of a man 6 feet 4 inches and 240 pounds, fled to the Baltimore 10-yard line, a full 88 yards away. When the clock was stopped, 19 seconds remained. On the next play, Starr hit Dowler at the back of the end zone, and the Packers were on their way.

"Hornung was great," remembers Unitas, who watched from the sidelines. "He had come all the way back to the form of the early nineteen sixties. He had always been one of the most talented offensive players in the history of the league, and he showed the size of his heart that day. He played with pain. And he played better than he ever had before."

Hornung scored twice more in the third quarter and added a fifth touchdown with less than 5 minutes to play and Green Bay in front by only 8 points. That put the game out of reach.

"I guess the reason I was able to do this," Hornung said, "is Vince Lombardi. Coach has a way of getting extra out of a player. If he told me to run into the stands and start selling programs, I wouldn't even question it. I'd be sure we would get a touchdown out of it, somehow."

The Packers had their league lead. All they had to do was win their last game, in San Francisco against the 49ers.

They did not. A touchdown pass from John Brodie to Vern Burke in the closing seconds gave San Francisco a 24–24 tie. Since the Colts had won their final game, the teams emerged from the grueling schedule with identical 10–3–1 records. There would have to be a playoff.

The next day, the Colts learned that Gary Cuozzo had suffered a shoulder separation and would need immediate surgery. Now not only was Unitas, the master, out of action, but so also was his talented replacement.

Don Shula, Baltimore's head coach, tried to sign up a veteran named Ed Brown, but the NFL rules would not allow a man to play in a postseason game unless he had been on the regular roster for at least the last two games. The Colts would have to meet the mighty Packers—in Green Bay, no less—without a professional quarterback.

Shula made his decision out of dire necessity. He went with his halfback Tom Matte, who thought he had ended his quarterbacking career at Ohio State. Matte was a sound halfback, a dedicated worker who made the most of less-than-spectacular physical gifts. But he was no quarterback. The Colts were pitied, and were given no chance at all to win.

Matte, a friendly, constantly smiling athlete, made the best of it. "Unitas says if I do too well, he'll stop talking to me," Matte joked, "so I suppose we won't have much to say any longer. I expect to beat the Packers. After all, a kid from Ohio State has all the advantages, doesn't he?"

It was December 26, 1965, and the winner of the game was going to draw the right to be host to the Cleveland Browns, Eastern Conference champions again, the next week in the NFL championship game.

The very nature of the Colts' team was enough to make Lombardi wary. "The thing is," he explained the night before the game, "we have to be ready for all different kinds of attack. We have a big problem, because we do not know what they're going to do. I mean, we all know Matte will be the quarterback. But what kind of a quarterback is he? What sort of plays will they run? Will the adversity of their situation make them play together more than ever, make them tougher to beat?"

Lombardi's worries were justified. The game became the longest ever played in the NFL. At the gun, the score was tied, 10–10. There would have to be a sudden-death overtime period. In that fifth quarter, the Colts fought their way to the Green Bay 47. Shula, seeing a chance to end it all, sent in Lou Michaels to try the long field goal. Michaels missed. The teams slogged on. At 13:39, the Pack had gotten to the Baltimore 25, and in came Don Chandler. He kicked it up–and over. That was it: Green Bay 13, Baltimore 10.

Green Bay had lost Starr with a rib injury on the very first play of the game. Starr aimed a pass at Bill Anderson, his tight end, who caught the ball and then fumbled it when hit by the cornerback Lenny Lyles. Don Shinnick, linebacker, picked up the ball and ran it over, making the score 7–0 for the Colts with 31 seconds gone. Starr, attempting to make the stop at the goal line, was blocked out by a Baltimore safety, Jim Welch. Starr was hurt.

It was time, suddenly, for the old veteran Zeke Bratkowski to come in. The Brat, who had seen years of action with Los Angeles and Chicago, had played hardly at all for the Packers. He was the insurance, and on this day his policy came due.

A column I wrote for my newspaper about Bratkowski's big day went, in part:

"As the echoing explosions of the victory set off wild celebrations throughout frigid Green Bay Sunday night, Zeke Bratkowski sat in the Packers' dressing room and smiled. His large, pulpy nose was bloodied; he had a welt on his right cheekbone, and his legs were scraped and raw.

"But he wore the biggest grin he was able to fit between the bruises and the scars of past wars. He had just won a Western Conference championship for the Packers.

" 'This was my biggest game,' he glowed, 'my biggest. It just had to be. I came in and tried to follow Bart's game plan. I expected them to blitz a lot, so I used blitz-type passes. You know, quickies to the side or over the middle.

" 'Anderson, Dale, and Dowler did so well that I had to look good. What a game.'

"But it was more than that. It was mostly the play of the thirty-four-year-old 'second-best' quarterback who has been kicked around from Chicago to Los Angeles to Green Bay and all the points in between.

"It was Bratkowski who completed twenty-two of thirty-nine passes for 248 yards, and it was Bratkowski as much as Anderson or Don Chandler or Paul Hornung or Ray Nitschke who won that overtime chiller.

" 'When Bart didn't get up,' Zeke remembered, 'I knew I was going in. All I remember is that I thought that now it's all up to me, all the responsibility and all the money and the championship . . . all mine. My stomach started to churn.'

" 'They were blitzing,' Zeke added, 'but we knew they might. I had a hell of an idea they would when I went in. They could have opened the game with another quick one. So I went to Billy [Anderson] for those short ones.'

"Brat cut down his drop many times, taking only two or three mincing steps before wheeling into the teeth of a blitz, and firing. And Anderson was there. Or Dowler. Or Dale. Playing a zone defense, the Colts couldn't get up in time to cut off the ball.

"Zeke was a second-round draft pick up by the Bears in 1953. He joined the Rams in 1960 and came to the Packers in 1963, midway through the season. Never was he a starter, always carrying a label that said 'inconsistent' or 'erratic' or 'choke.'

"But this year he saved four games for the Packers with clutch passes and guts calls, and in the process convinced Coach Vince Lombardi that he was not lacking, simply untried.

" 'I never felt shaky about sending Zeke in once I saw what he had. He's got a world of experience; he's smart and he's not afraid of any defense. He doesn't hear footsteps and he doesn't get rid of the ball just to avoid getting belted.

" 'We like that here in Green Bay.'

"So Zeke Bratkowski has found a home at age thirty-four. He plays for a team whose coach says 'desire is hatred.' He plays behind an offensive line called the best in the business. He has runners like Jim Taylor and Paul Hornung, who may not be what they were, but who are still a damn sight better than most."

After the game, Lombardi called it the toughest a team of his had ever been in. "It was football as it should be played," he said, using one of his favorite superlatives. "A tremendous hitting game."

The New York Times correspondent saw it this way: "It was a thrilling bit of fantasy . . . all the way to the abrupt termination by Chandler's winning field goal. The game was brutal and bruising, waged without quarter and with a furious, baleful intensity. Tension kept mounting steadily until spectators almost got the screamy-meemies. This had to be one of the great television shows of the year. It certainly was one of the great football games of this or any year."

What it was, was Lombardi football. Tough and unyielding. "This game pointed out, I think, for all time the value of conditioning," Lombardi said later. "The Packers did not tire. They did not fall victim to fatigue. They played as hard in that overtime period as they did in the first quarter. In fact, they played better, harder. They were in the best shape any men could ever achieve, and it won a championship for them."

There was now a week to go before the NFL championship game with Cleveland. Several reporters, including myself, now found themselves stranded in Green Bay. Our home offices had decided it would be more economical to pay a week's hotel bill than the additional air fare.

Therefore, when the game ended and the stories had been written and filed, a disconsolate handful of visiting sportswriters made their way through the ice and snow, accompanied by wind and dropping temperatures. We checked back into the

Northland Hotel. It was Sunday night. It was cold. The towns-people, still sky-high with their victory, were continuing their celebrations of success.

What began for us then was a week of the Green Bay life, a week in the Northland Hotel, a week with Vince Lombardi. That first night the hotel manager had to be found and roused so that the dining room might be opened. All during the week there were no more than a dozen or so guests in the hotel, all of them—us—newsmen. Memory insists that among those who stayed were Milton Gross of *The New York Post*, Dave Eisenberg of *The New York Journal-American*, Jimmy Cannon of the Hearst Newspaper Syndicate, Bill Gleason of *Chicago's American,* Bud Lea of *The Milwaukee Sentinel,* Chuck Johnson of *The Milwaukee Journal*, Harold Rosenthal of *The New York Herald Tribune*, and myself.

Each day we would bravely arise, bravely shower, even more bravely try the Northland's breakfast menu, and then begin the trek to Lambeau Field. We talked to the players, to the coaches, to the equipment men. We competed with one another to come up with a new question, and even the players began to appreciate the humor of our trapped situation.

But not Vince Lombardi. He had never been exposed to a week of sportswriters, poking and prying around, cluttering up his locker room, dancing on the sidelines to avoid the cold that nipped at feet and fingers.

After three or four days, I thought I'd ask Lombardi to compare the way he prepared for the Colts with the way he was now preparing for Cleveland. You did not simply prepare for the invasion of Jimmy Brown, it might be remembered. You attacked the problem with zeal and gusto and determination and the certainty that it would not help.

So I began to pose the question. "Coach, now that you are preparing for the Browns, how is it different from the way you prepared for the Colts?"

He fixed me with that Lombardi glare. "The Colts' game is over," he said. "I don't have time to talk about that."

I fidgeted. "But, Coach, they are two entirely different teams, and I thought it might be interesting to get a comparison."

Lombardi zapped me again with that stare. "I said we don't talk about Baltimore anymore," he growled.

I was accustomed to other coaches' answering all sorts of questions, some hardly relevant. "You're rude, Coach," I blustered. "I'm only trying to do a job."

Lombardi turned to Harold Rosenthal of *The Herald Tribune,* whom he had known from his New York days. "Harold, who is this kid?" he asked. "Teach him to ask a question."

That did it. "Mister Lombardi, I won't bother you again," I said. "I'll ask my questions of people with the ability to answer them."

Slowly he turned to me for a long moment. Then suddenly he smiled. "You'll do, kid," he said, "but please don't ask any more stupid questions, okay?" And he proceeded to outline the comparison—in far more detail than I either expected or was capable of comprehending.

And so the week went. One night at dinner in Wally's Spot, a restaurant that has since, lamentably, been razed, Milton Gross turned to his table companions and said, "I can't wait for Sunday's game to be over."

"Why?" someone asked. "So you can go home?"

"Not really," Gross smiled. "I'm curious to see if they really give you ten bucks and a new suit when you get released."

It was that kind of week.

Dave Robinson, the outstanding linebacker who was a transplanted New Jerseyite, still made his home in the Garden State. One day after practice he announced that he was leaving for home Monday morning, and asked if I would like to go with him.

"Sure," I said, somewhat flattered. "What time is your plane leaving?"

"No, not a plane," Davey grinned. "I'm driving. Figure it should take us two days. How about it?"

I giggled nervously. "Two days? On the highways here? In all that snow? And ice? No, I'll walk—I mean, I'll fly."

Somehow, Sunday arrived, and with it a four-inch snowstorm. All week the weather had been relatively mild—for Green Bay. The temperatures during the day were sometimes as high as twenty degrees. But now it was snowing heavily. The switchboard operator at the Northland, calling as requested at eight o'clock, had this to say:

"Good morning, Packer backer. It is eight o'clock. The temperature is eleven degrees, and it is snowing on game day."

Lombardi did not like the turn of the weather. "Jim Brown can run on anything," he told one of his assistant coaches. "Our men need good football. I don't want to have to win this game in the air. We'll run, if we can."

Lombardi's runners of course, were Taylor and Hornung. Starr was able to start at quarterback, with Dowler, Dale, and Bill Anderson the receivers. The offensive line, tackle to tackle, was unchanged—Skoronski, Thurston, Bowman, Kramer, and Gregg.

Cleveland's weapons, aside from the impossible Jim Brown, were Paul Warfield, Gary Collins, and John Brewer as the receivers, and Frank Ryan, the quarterback with the doctor's degree in advanced mathematics (Ryan, now retired from football, heads a government computer-programming center in Washington, D.C.).

The snow stopped shortly after the game began, and the field turned into a sea of grasping mud. As expected, the runners had difficulty—the Cleveland runners. Brown was held to 50 yards in a dozen carries, while Ernie Green, the halfback, was able to manage only 5 yards in three tries.

Hornung was superb, rushing for 105 yards in eighteen carries, with one burst of 34 yards. Taylor was almost as effective, with 96 yards in twenty-seven tries.

Starr completed ten of eighteen passes for 147 yards and a 47-yard touchdown toss to Dale. Cleveland's Frank Ryan was eight for eighteen, for 115 yards and a touchdown.

But the story of the game was Green Bay's relentless ball control. The Packers ran sixty-nine offensive plays, to thirty-nine for Cleveland, an unusually high advantage. The score was 23–12, with the Packers scoring 10 points in the second half while holding the Browns scoreless.

It was a splendid victory through adversity. Several of Lombardi's players were severely injured. There was Starr, of course, who had been a mere spectator a week earlier. There was Taylor, who had a severely pulled back muscle. Dowler had a twisted ankle and both shoulders wrenched. Hornung was gimpy. Several of the defensive players, notably Nitschke and Kostelnik, were nursing aches and bruises.

But they played. "I think," said Taylor after the game, "that we might not have been able to play for another team today. Coach Lombardi has spent much time teaching us that pain is a condition to be disregarded. It was burned into our brains, and we never really doubted we'd play. No matter what, we'd play."

The offensive line worked away at the Cleveland defense. Steadily, using the power sweep and the off-tackle drive, the Packers forced the Browns into backward steps. It was a fatal mistake for the Browns. Once they began to overcompensate for the run, Starr picked them to death with his short passes. Dowler caught five for 59 yards, Dale two for 60. It was a methodically conducted execution, and Cleveland's head coach, Blanton Collier, was the first to admit it when it was all over.

"They beat us by keeping the ball and making no mistakes," he said. "We just weren't as tough as the Packers."

Green Bay had come back to the top of the football world, and had done it in dramatic style. The year before, Baltimore and Cleveland had played for the NFL championship, and Cleveland had won. So the Packers took care of the Colts in the playoff game and then the Browns in the title game.

The weather was a handicap and the injuries played a major part in the pregame figuring. But Lombardi knew it all along. "We had the best team," he said, "and if we played our kind of football, I promised them they'd have another championship."

The Packers were about to enter another golden period, which came about when the National Football League and the American Football League agreed on merger plans. They announced the creation of a championship game, matching the two league winners. Lamar Hunt, owner and president of the AFL's Kansas City Chiefs, called it the Super Bowl.

The first one would be played between the winners of the 1966 league races.

Football Capital of
the World

THE WAR BETWEEN THE LEAGUES HAD BEEN EXPENSIVE. No team could afford to go on forever paying one hundred times the value of a rookie. The team owners, practical above all else, finally realized that they had gotten on a slide to nowhere.

The American Football League had been founded in 1960, but for its first five years was hardly competition for the firmly established National Football League. Then came a multi-million-dollar television contract for the AFL, and suddenly it had the money to bid against the NFL for the best players coming out of the college ranks.

The result was a bonanza if you happened to be a graduating football star who wanted to play in the pros. It was a nightmare if you owned a professional football team. In one celebrated case, the AFL's New York Jets had to offer $400,000 to get a University of Alabama quarterback named Joe Namath.

The Green Bay organization was caught in this squeeze more than most teams, because of its unique structure. Lombardi was forced to pay out a million dollars to two rookie running backs on the 1966 roster—$600,000 to Donnie Anderson, a sweet-moving, swivel-hipped halfback out of Texas Tech, and $400,000 to Jim Grabowski, a heavy-legged, punishing fullback from Illinois. It was simply too much, and Lombardi became one of those fighting to bring the leagues together.

There were other men more involved with the merger solution, but they had no duties on the field or as a general manager and head coach. The most influential parties were Tex Schramm, president and general manager of the Dallas Cowboys, George Halas, owner and president of the Chicago Bears, and Lamar Hunt, owner-president of the Kansas City Chiefs, along with Commissioner Pete Rozelle and his chief aide, Jim Kensil.

Lombardi resented the first-year men because of their extravagant bonus contracts, but learned to respect them for being able to take advantage of the situation. He felt sorry for the older players, who had been born too early and missed out on the windfall.

On several occasions, it all made Lombardi lose his patience. There was one time, for instance at the Green Bay table during a draft meeting. The Packers had made up their minds on a choice for that round. But, not wishing to waste it on a boy who might be inclined toward the AFL, Lombardi had a call placed to the athlete's home.

"This is Vince Lombardi of the Green Bay Packers," he said. "We want to draft you right now, and we want to know what it will take to sign you."

"Golly, Coach, this is great. I was hoping you'd call me," the player responded. "Are we ready to talk terms?"

"Ready," sighed Lombardi.

"Well, I want a fifty-thousand dollar bonus," the collegian began.

"Done," said Lombardi.

"And I want a two-year, no-cut contract," he added.

"Done," said Lombardi.

"And I want enough extra money for a Toronado," the boy said.

"What the hell," Lombardi yelled, "is a Toronado?"

"It's a sports car, Coach," the player whispered, somewhat fearful.

"You," said Lombardi, "are a stupid young man. You should have simply asked for five thousand more on your bonus. I will not be blackmailed. You will never get a Toronado from me. That's final."

He slammed down the receiver, drafted the player anyway and knew full well the kid would sign. He did.

The necessary legislation for approval of the merger was granted by the Congress of the United States on October 21, 1966, and the Super Bowl was born.

"When Lombardi heard there would be a Super Bowl," said the quick-witted Steve Wright, then a Green Bay offensive tackle, "he decided the Packers would be the NFL's representative in it. I mean, he just decided it. We didn't have any choice. He told us in summer camp. 'You men,' he said, 'will be playing a bit longer this season. But it will be made worth your while, I suspect. Just don't disappoint me.' He wanted the Super Bowl, but not for the money. He wanted to be the one to make it for the first time. Coach never could stand finishing second."

Wright, a carefree, fun-loving graduate of the University of Alabama, had a special kind of arrangement with Lombardi. "He knew I was going to make jokes," Steve says, "and he knew I knew he didn't much like it. But he let me do it. Oh, I got to him a few times. I'm the guy who came out of the game after blowing a block, the guy he got so mad that he started punching on the chest.

"Now, I'm six feet five, and I don't think Coach was any more than five eight or so. I weighed two hundred sixty pounds, and he couldn't have been two hundred. It was kind of ludicrous, but I didn't know what to do. Should I have just stood there? The whole team was laughing, and I felt kind of silly. Should I have walked away? I could have hit him back, but I'm not that stupid. It was embarrassing, really. The man was so intense about winning he felt I let him down by making one mistake.

"I remember once, I think it was the nineteen sixty-five season, when Gregg was hurt and I filled in. He was going over game films on a Tuesday morning, and every time he found a mistake by Steve Wright he'd stop the camera, reel it back, play it again, reel it back, over and over and over. Finally he turned on the lights and looked at me.

" 'Wright,' he said, 'you'll be a star someday. If they invent a position called rotten tackle.' "

Wright went to the Washington Redskins after spending a season with the Giants, to whom Lombardi had sent him in a trade. "We were honest to God afraid to smoke in front of him," Wright remembers. "But the best I ever saw happened one night during training camp. We had worked our butts off all day, and then sat through meetings after dinner, and we had maybe an hour to kill before curfew. So Bob Skoronski and I walked to town and bought ice cream cones. Then we started walking back to the camp. Big deal, right? Well, I finished my cone first, and we were just strollin' along, talking, when Bob spied Coach coming toward us from about a quarter of a mile away. Next thing I know, Skoronski dumps his ice cream cone behind some bushes. I asked him why he did that.

" 'Steve,' he said, 'I know Coach says it's okay for us to eat ice cream, but I'm afraid he'll think I'm not training right and he'll work me harder tomorrow. Don't tell anybody what I did, okay?' "

No one was more aware of Lombardi's grip on his players than Bart Starr. "I have been called a robot," he said, "and if it is true, then I'm proud of it. I learned more football from Coach Lombardi than would have been possible under any other man. He had to tear down everything I had learned previously and then fill me with the right thoughts, the proper theories. You know, some of the greatest years I guess I ever spent were those under Lombardi. So many things I learned. He was a most unusual man, and sometimes misunderstood. I know he is credited with saying 'Winning isn't everything; it's the only thing.'

"I suppose in the stories, the legends they tell about him, Lombardi would sound like that. It would sound like the way he would say it. But it wasn't what he really said. The real statement is: 'Winning isn't everything; it's how you react to losing.' Lombardi always taught us that pro football wasn't the end, only the means to an end. Life is not just football alone. You'd hear these things, year after year, and then suddenly one day you'd tell yourself that these things are true, that they are real.

"Lombardi never accepted compromise, with himself or his players. He would drive us all week until there was nothing that could be unexpected, and the playing on Sunday would be the easiest part of the week. But a man must have goals established for himself. He must have dreams, desires, ambitions. These are the mechanisms for striving. But there is a price that must be paid for these. Nothing of value is free. You have to earn your own self-respect.

"Lombardi had a sheer, flaming, burning desire to excel, and I don't see anything wrong in this. There is nothing wrong in wanting to be a champion, or trying to be one. It's fashionable to downgrade the champion these days, or anyway, the guy who wants to be one. We are, in our society, fast losing track of teamwork. Yet I don't feel that any man can make it alone, any more than you can live without loyalty—or dreams. I think there is more of a need for these in our society."

The speaker might have been Lombardi himself. Starr had been a ragtag quarterback with an erratic arm when Vince found him on the Green Bay bench, a seventeenth-round draft choice out of Alabama. Lombardi made Starr a winner.

"He started me in the last four games of the nineteen fifty-nine season," Bart remembers. "I was behind Lamar McHan and Babe Parilli before that, and I didn't have the faintest idea of what a professional quarterback had to learn.

"Vince built the Packers around execution. He kept it simple. He even told us his offense was for simple-minded people. We never attempted to do a lot of nifty ball-handling or tried to fool the defense. We merely attempted to establish a sound, fundamental game, where one fellow is pitted against another, and it becomes his responsibility to just root the opposition out, block him any way possible, and let the back adjust.

"The Lombardi system continually stressed a minimum of mistakes. Mistakes on the football field beat you, and he constantly pounded away at us that we could not afford mistakes. Coach Lombardi's mental and physical approach to the game was as follows: Physical toughness by you will make the opponents weaken, and mental toughness by you will make them crack.

"I got to thinking about it later, and the man was a very emotional person. He was spurred to anger or to tears almost equally easily. He would get misty-eyed, and he actually cried at times, and no one thought less of him for crying."

Another articulate observer is Jerry Kramer, who has collaborated in writing books about the Green Bay days with Dick Schaap. "Coach never takes second place when it comes to faith healers," Jerry has said. "He could just walk into a training room filled with injured players and say: 'What the hell is wrong with you guys? There's nobody in here hurt.' And the dressing room would clear immediately. All the wounded would be healed."

When Kramer's *Instant Replay* was published, he gave a copy to everyone connected with the team except Lombardi. He was afraid of Vince's reaction to it. Several weeks later, Mrs. Lombardi walked up to Jerry and asked for a book.

"I've been meaning to give you one," Kramer stammered, "if you promise not to show Vince that line about the short, fat Italian." Kramer says he worked for a week on the inscription for Vince's copy, and finally wrote: *To Vince Lombardi, against whom I and all others shall forever be measured.*

The next week, Vince and Marie and several friends bumped into Kramer in a hotel elevator. "Jerry," Marie said, "I just loved the book. It's marvelous. I enjoyed it tremendously. It has helped me to understand."

"What," Kramer asked, "me or football?"

"Him," she said, pointing to Vince. "After twenty-eight years it has helped me to understand him. He liked it, too."

Trying to understand Lombardi is an activity many have engaged in. Henry Jordan, the all-pro defensive tackle, is one of them.

"Lombardi chews you out, and you don't like it," Jordan says, recalling a moment of insight he once had. "You love him and you hate him in turn, but you always respect him. One time at a meeting, he got on our offensive guards something awful. It was so bad everybody came out of the meeting objecting. We were saying to each other: 'He's got no right to talk like that.' I can remember there was a group of us talking that way, and just then we passed another room.

"We looked in, and there were the two guards, and already they had their playbooks open and were studying. Then it hit me: Lombardi was right. He had a message to give, and he got it across. He's aloof from the players. We don't really know him as a man. It's like the army. We're the troops, and he's the general. He runs a tight ship, on and off the field, and he's right. If he'd give us an inch we would take a mile."

Carroll Dale is another one of the troops who likes to talk about his general. "I remember one of the first things he told the team in nineteen sixty-five—my first year with the Packers —was that there should be only three things important to us: One, our church or religion; two, our family; and three, Green Bay Packer football—in that order of importance. He also taught us humility and gratitude. We always knelt together and repeated the Lord's Prayer after a victory, realizing that we were fortunate to win. In the years that I spent with the Packers, I came to respect and admire Coach Lombardi not only as a coach but as a real man. He always reminded us that football was similar to many phases of life—the competition, the successes and failures, and the respect and consideration for others, both teammates and opponents. He told us not to make excuses when we lost, and to have pride in our organization, pride in our personal performance, and to have determination and dedication strong enough to keep us going when we lost or got knocked back.

"He has said—publicly, of course—that members of the 1966 Packers had love and respect for each other . . . he often reminded us that we were dependent on each other and that we won or lost as a team. I think he was as rough, tough, and as hardnosed as any coach I have ever known . . . yet he was interested in developing better men of us all, for certainly he realized it took real men to win consistently in the NFL and to win the game of life."

The last of Lombardi's years of Green Bay glory began with that 1966 season. The Packers won twelve of their fourteen games, losing only to Minnesota, 20–17, and to San Francisco, 21–20. Four points kept the Pack from an undefeated season. "We made mistakes in both those games," Lombardi is recalled to have said, "mistakes that cost us victory. We should have won everything this year; it was that good a team."

But Green Bay won far more than necessary for another conference championship. The Baltimore Colts were a distant second with a 9–5 showing. Green Bay scored 335 points and allowed only 163. Starr emerged as the NFL's leading passer, completing 156 in 251 attempts for 2,257 yards and fourteen touchdowns. He was intercepted only three times.

Jim Taylor gained 705 yards in 204 carries and scored four touchdowns rushing. Elijah Pitts added 393 yards, and Hornung, who played in only nine games, had 200 yards. Taylor also finished as the team's leading receiver, catching forty-one passes for 331 yards and two more touchdowns. Dale, however, was the long ball threat, hauling in thirty-seven of Starr's passes for 876 yards and seven touchdowns.

Bob Jeter and Dave Robinson shared team interception honors with five each. Herb Adderley and Tom Brown had four, Lee Roy Caffey and Willie Wood three, Ray Nitschke two. The Packers were second in interceptions, with twenty-eight, and led in interception yardage returned, with 547, as well as in touchdowns resulting from interceptions, with six.

Meanwhile, in the Eastern Conference, a new football power was emerging in Dallas. The expansionist Cowboys were coached by Tom Landry, the former associate of Lombardi under Jim Lee Howell in New York. Landry had drilled his talent-laden squad in an intricate system of offense and defense. Landry had always been an egghead type of coach. Even in his assistant coaching days with the Giants, he established a reputation as a man of complex theory.

Landry's ideas worked. He is a man of infinite patience, preferring to wait for his athletes to absorb the theory. The Cowboys began in 1960, when they played a dozen games and emerged with nothing more than a tie for their efforts. But the nucleus was there, with the quarterback Don Meredith, the fullback Don Perkins, Bob Lilly, defensive tackle, and others who would play a large role in making a championship team.

It took Landry six seasons, with constant changing of peripheral personnel, but he never wavered from his philosophy of coaching. It was diametrically opposed to Lombardi's. Landry believed that intricacy confused the opposition, while insisting that intelligent players would not become bogged down with the detail of the system. Lombardi, on the other hand said: "The less they must remember, the better they are. If you can do a few simple things well, you have all you need to win."

Dallas, which had been second to the Browns in 1965, exploded all over the Southwest in 1966, winning ten of fourteen games, tying another and finishing with a 10–3–1 record. The offense scored more points than any other team in either league, 445, while the defense allowed only 239 points, the lowest figure in the Eastern Conference.

The Cowboys compared well against Vince's Packers, who had lost to them in an exhibition game that summer. The offense was flashy, with Meredith throwing to receivers like Bob Hayes and Lance Rentzel. Perkins and Dan Reeves handled the running. And the defense was dotted with standouts like Lilly, Willie Townes at tackle, George Andrie, end, the linebackers Chuck Howley, Lee Roy Jordan and Dave Edwards, and the deep backs Mel Renfro, Mike Gaechter, and Cornell Green.

The game was played in the Cotton Bowl, before an overflow crowd of more than 75,000. Everyone knew that beyond gaining the league championship, the winner would represent the NFL in the first Super Bowl, to be played two weeks later in the Los Angeles Coliseum. Both teams were capable and confident of beating the American Football League's champion, but neither would predict victory in this game.

"Dallas presents more of a problem to us than any team we have played this season," Lombardi said. "The offense can score on any play. The Cowboys do not have to play ball-control football to win. They cannot fall too far behind, either, because with their passing game, no lead is safe against them. And the defense is as tough as any in the league. This team will be heard from for a long time, and just because this is the first championship game for the Cowboys means nothing. They can beat us easily."

Landry was even grimmer. "We're young and unsure of ourselves," he offered, "and compared to the Packers' experience, we're novices at pressure games. Green Bay never lets up. You're unable to relax for a minute. They can score from any point on the field, and if they do get a lead, their ball-control can eat up the clock. They make you play their kind of game, and if it gets to that, only they can win."

Privately, Landry told his team what he expected. "If you must give up the ball, make sure it happens after you score. Don't let them hold it. We need points almost every time we take possession, because they're going to chunk it out and get over the goal line eventually. Only we can't afford to wait before we get it back."

Meredith gave Landry and the Cowboys a frantic time early in the week, when he was rushed to a Dallas hospital with what were described as severe stomach pains. It turned out to be nothing more than nerves, for the usually happy-go-lucky Meredith was wound up tighter than a watch spring. "I just suddenly realized how important the game was," he said later, "and I knew I had never played in one that big before. The mind can do strange things to the body."

But physicians assured Meredith he was all right, and would be able to play. He practiced Thursday, and was pronounced ready for action.

Lombardi, on the eve of the game, made a typical prediction. "If Starr has a hot day, we'll win," he said. "In this league it boils down to that most of the time. The team with the hot quarterback usually can win."

By the time the game started, Kansas City had already beaten Buffalo for the AFL championship. The Chiefs then sat back to witness the Cowboys and Packers slug it out for the right to become their opponents.

The game began as though Dallas were in the wrong stadium. The Packers quickly gained a 14–0 lead. There was a 76-yard drive capped by a Starr-to-Pitts touchdown pass. Then, just seconds later, the rookie fullback Jim Grabowski picked up a fumbled snap from center and took it over for another touchdown.

But the Cowboys rallied. Dan Reeves scored once from the 3-yard line, and then Perkins scored on a run of 23 yards, both before the first quarter was out. It was tied, 14–14, and the Packers quickly re-evaluated their opposition.

The half ended with Green Bay holding a tenuous 21–17 lead, after Starr had connected with Dale for a touchdown and Dallas countered with a field goal by Danny Villanueva. The Mexican-born place-kicker added another early in the third quarter, and Dallas had moved to within a point of the Packers, 21–20.

But Starr, who was to complete nineteen of the twenty-eight passes he attempted, struck again in the third quarter with a long one to Boyd Dowler, making it 28–20, and then, in the fourth quarter, added another strike to Max McGee. The fact that Don Chandler missed the extra point after McGee's touchdown seemed of little importance, for now the Packers held a 34–20 lead with scant moments remaining in the game. A Green Bay victory seemed assured.

Except Dallas did not figure it that way. Meredith stunned the Packers and drove the partisan crowd hysterical when he clicked with a 68-yard pass to his tight end, Frank Clarke, for a touchdown. Villanueva made the conversion. Now, as Lombardi gaped incredulously on the sidelines, the Packers were suddenly in trouble. Another Dallas touchdown would tie it up. That missed conversion by Chandler suddenly became very important.

Green Bay could not move when it took the ball, and was

forced to punt back to the Cowboys. Time remained for one drive. It was now or never, under the pressure of a championship game's final moments.

Two minutes showed on the clock when Clarke caught another Meredith pass for 21 yards, good to the Green Bay 21. Perkins ripped off 4 yards up the middle, to the Packers' 17. Now Meredith aimed for Clarke in the end zone, and missed, but the officials called the Packer safety Tom Brown for pass interference. Dallas had the ball on the Green Bay 2, with 1:52 left. A score would tie the game and send it into a sudden-death overtime.

Now it was defeaning. The Cotton Bowl seemed to shudder back and forth with the crescendo of noise generated by the fans. Reeves picked up a yard of the precious 2 on an off-tackle slant to the right. It seemed impossible for the Cowboys not to score now, and with their momentum and lightning-fast offense, they would hold the advantage in an extra period.

Meredith called for a rollout, a play in which he exercises a split-second option of passing or continuing downfield as a running back. He chose to throw. His substitute tight end, Pettis Norman, dropped the ball in the end zone. But the Dallas tackle Tony Liscio had been called for offsides, and now the Packers had some breathing room; Dallas was on the 6. Now Meredith faked a play-action pass, decoying the defense with a handoff to Perkins who hit the center of the line, then straightening up and throwing a flare pass to Reeves in the unguarded flat. It took enormous courage. And Reeves dropped the ball.

It was now third down. Meredith threw to Norman again, to the 2, but the end was immediately smacked out of bounds.

And now it was the moment of truth. One play was left to the Cowboys. It was fourth down and goal to go. No more chances, barring a Green Bay penalty. One more shot.

Hayes was sent in as a tight end, a position he seldom played. The idea was to isolate him on a cornerback, after he faked a block into the corner linebacker Dave Robinson. If Dallas could make the Packers think a sweep was coming, the cornerback would have to force the play by moving into the line. Then Meredith would lob a short one over his head and—if all went well—into Hayes's arms.

Hayes, the fastest man in pro football, forgot to block Robinson. He looped to the outside and cut across the end zone. He was clear. But so, too, was Robinson. The hulking linebacker zeroed in on Meredith and wrapped his arms around him. Meredith had to unload the ball, too quickly. He threw it high. Tom Brown leaped and caught it for a touchback. The ball game was over.

Green Bay won it, 34–27.

Characteristically, Lombardi singled out the defensive heroes Robinson and Brown for incorrect procedure on the crucial play.

Robinson, he said, should first have forced through the guard hole, to make Meredith hold back on his rollout plane, thus breaking up the flow of the play. But Dave went right for the quarterback.

Brown, he said, should have been covering Reeves, as the responsibility for him belonged to the first man out of the backfield. Brown was honest enough to admit: "I lost Reeves in the flow of the traffic. I didn't know where he was. I saw Hayes, and I saw Clarke, and I took up a position between them. I was right there when Meredith threw. I was a very lucky man."

The Cowboys were disconsolate. Meredith, especially, was in tears when the team went to its dressing room. "All right there, and I blew it," he said. "We had four shots to go two yards. I outsmarted myself. We should have kept running. I'm not sure if I'll ever get over this, because it was all my fault."

Thus the Green Bay Packers had a second straight league championship. And they were headed for Los Angeles and the confrontation with a team from the American Football

League. It would be the first such battle on the field after many in the courts, and the excitement it generated is now part of American sports lore.

The Kansas City Chiefs had reacted impulsively after their victory at Buffalo. "Bring on the Packers. We'll tear 'em apart," said their defensive back Fred Williamson, who was called "the Hammer" for his forearm smashes to prospective pass receivers. "No contest," he insisted. "Now we get to prove it."

"We will tear up the Packers," said the Kansas City head coach, Hank Stram. "We are much the better team."

Lombardi, when told of this statement, simply smiled. "Good for Stram," he said. "If he had said anything else, I wouldn't have any respect for him. Whether he believes it or not."

Lombardi now had a difficult decision. Hornung was at the end of his career, owing to a painful nerve in his neck, which was affecting his spinal column. But after all the years in which Paul had meant so much to the Packers, Vince was hesitant to keep him on the bench.

"I had a great conflict within myself," Lombardi said later. "After all, it was the first Super Bowl, and Paul, with the great years and great performances he had contributed to the Packers, deserved as much as, or more than, anyone to have the honor of playing in it. But a jamming blow on his head would give him excruciating pain and might injure him much more seriously.

"I had seen too many movies of Paul flinching on a block. This was not from any lack of courage; Hornung possessed all the courage any ball player needs. I just couldn't stomach it, and I don't think Hornung could, either.

"I had the thought that, if things went badly for us early in the game, if we did not dominate as we should, I might have had to use Hornung to give us a lift. As it turned out . . . when, late in the game, I asked Paul if he wanted to go in, he said: 'No, Coach, it's all over.' "

The Packers and the Chiefs had two weeks to prepare, and

Lombardi often commented that they were the strangest two weeks he had ever experienced.

"In the two weeks we had to get ready, every owner in the league called me on the telephone at least once or wrote to try to express what this game meant. It wasn't only Packer prestige on the line, but that of the whole NFL. We had everything to lose and nothing to gain.

"We had never seen Kansas City play but we did exchange three game films. Even then, we could not rate them precisely because we were not familiar with their AFL opposition. But, going into that game, there was one thing I firmly believed. Technically, there was no way they could beat the Green Bay Packers if my team went out and played its kind of football. There was only one chance in twenty-five of us losing, but that, too, is what makes this a game for madmen.

"We could see that Kansas City was weak at cornerback and that the stacked defenses—linebackers behind linemen and dealing to one side or the other to confuse offensive blocking—would make them difficult to run against. At the same time, however, it would make their cornerbacks even more vulnerable.

"On the other hand, we saw that they liked to rotate their defenses toward the strength of the offensive formation. With that defensive alignment, the Chiefs could not possibly stop our passing game; so we concentrated on that and kept our running game simple."

One of the NFL owners, Cleveland's Arthur Modell, was supremely confident about resting the league's prestige in Lombardi's hands. "Vince Lombardi," he said, "is without a doubt the greatest coach in the history of professional football. If I wanted to win one game, just one, I would have to have Lombardi as the coach. Then I would not need a superhuman team. He is capable of extracting superhuman efforts from ordinary men. I feel very badly for the Kansas City Chiefs, for they feel they have a real chance at winning this game. They do not, and they never had, and they never will."

Kansas City brought a solid club into the Los Angeles Coliseum on Super Sunday, January 15, 1967. Len Dawson was the quarterback, with Mike Garrett and Curtis McClinton the runners, Otis Taylor and Chris Burford the wide receivers, Fred Arbanas the tight end, and an interior line of Jim Tyrer and Dave Hill at tackle, Ed Budde and Curt Merz at guard, and Wayne Frazier, center. Defensively, the front four was composed of Jerry Mays and Chuck Hurston at the ends, Andy Rise and Buck Buchanan at the tackles. Sherrill Headrick was the middle linebacker, flanked by Bobby Bell and E.J. Holub. The deep men were Williamson and Willie Mitchell, cornerbacks, Bobby Hunt and Johnny Robinson, safeties.

The Packers scored in the first quarter, on a 37-yard pass from Starr to McGee, a play in which old Max, filling in for the injured Boyd Dowler, reached behind him as he fled across the goal line and took in the slightly errant throw one-handed.

In the second period, Kansas City scored and it looked as though the Chiefs might make good on all their boasts. McClinton rammed home from the 7, and then Mike Mercer added a 31-yard field goal. But the Packers had already scored again, on a 14-yard Green Bay sweep by Jim Taylor, and the half ended at 14–10.

Green Bay turned the game around early in the third quarter, when Dawson, intending to throw to his tight end, became confused with the Packers' reaction on defense and threw to the wrong spot. It was the right spot for Willie Wood, who caught the ball on the Green Bay 45 and returned it 50 yards, to the Kansas City 5. Pitts needed only one play to slash through left tackle, and with 2:27 gone in the second half, the score was 21–10.

McGee was to catch another Starr touchdown pass, of 13 yards, and Pitts was to score again on an even shorter run. At the end it was 35–10, and Kansas City was humiliated. So, too, was the Hammer. Williamson had to be carried off the field unconscious in the fourth quarter, after he had tried to tackle Donny Anderson on a sweep and found three men waiting for him. When asked why the Packers had waited so long to silence the braggart Williamson, Lombardi snapped: "Because it was the first time he was near a play, that's why."

Lombardi, caught up in the headiness of victory, was less than kind to the Chiefs after the game. "In my opinion, the Chiefs don't rate with the top teams in the National Football League," he offered. "They're a good football team with fine speed, but I'd have to say NFL football is tougher. Dallas is a better team, and so are several others. We actually had to make very few adjustments in the second half. Our game plan was basically sound, and we stayed with it. The difference was that we played more aggressively, and that's all. I told them to start tackling and stop grabbing. I think their defense hurt them. They play a stack, which is not a sound defense, in that they can't rush the passer very well. We used more passes because they were daring us to throw."

Then, the final stab. "This wasn't one of our most solid games, but Starr was outstanding, as he's been all along."

Indeed, Starr was. He completed sixteen of twenty-three passing attempts for 250 yards. Seven times he found McGee, who gained 138 yards and scored two touchdowns. McGee also administered a lesson on football to the Kansas City cornerback Willie Mitchell. It was a shock treatment the youngster could never forget, and he became gun-shy.

Starr tried to be kinder, but even his disdain crept through. "They're a fine football team, but their defense was not that tough. We've seen it before. Detroit used a similar defense against us, and we knew pretty well what to do."

Stram was crushed. "We played well in the first half and at the start of the second half. The interception changed the personality of the game. You don't like to say that one play did that much, but it seemed to. They are an excellent team, and it is imperative not to give them anything easy. We did, and it cost us. Starr was terrific all afternoon, making the big third-down play. Somebody said he hit seven of nine third downs in the first half and five of seven in the second. That's fantastic. We were in a variety of coverages, but he seemed to hit the right areas to keep key dives alive. We thought we had a pretty good team, and we still think so, but the Packers are great."

Jerry Mays, the Chiefs' co-captain, said: "It hurts more than I thought it would. It's bad enough when you let yourself down, but when you let the whole league down, it sure hurts. All the talking is over now. They beat us on the grass. They beat us physically. They're a great ball club, the best we've played. That's hard to say, but I suppose it's true. They're sure as heck as good as any we've played. What takes the heart out of you is how Starr just stands back there and hits those third-down passes. They had some patterns where they had maybe half a step on our coverage, and he put the ball right there."

McGee, who had caught only four passes all season, announced his retirement in the locker room after the game. Then he was asked if it would stick. "I guess it's really up to Coach," he said. "Last year I said I retired, then he called me in May and told me I had made a mistake, that I hadn't retired after all. He was right."

Max did not retire. Lombardi phoned him in the spring and told him to report to the training camp at Saint Norbert's College, and old Max was there.

But Hornung and Taylor had played their last game as members of the Green Bay Packers.

Paul had been told by the doctors not to play. He had been told they could not guarantee his condition—permanently—should he suffer another injury to the spine or neck. He knew this and so did Lombardi, and Vince spent the winter soul-searching. The NFL had created a new team, in New Orleans, and each existing team was to make available a list of veterans who could be claimed by the Saints. A certain number were allowed to be "frozen" or protected, and the others were fair game.

Finally, Lombardi decided to place Paul's name on the list. But he made it clear to the Saints, who were to be coached by a Lombardi assistant, Tom Fears, that Paul could not play again. "It was one of the most difficult things I ever had to do," Vince said.

"I gave up Hornung because there was no way out of it," Lombardi said in a national magazine article. "It was the saddest day I have known in Green Bay. I was crying when I told him. There will never be another number five on the Packers. I told him that, too. We had to put eleven men on the list, and because Paul had a pinched nerve in his neck that could cause paralysis of his left side, we didn't think anyone would take him. It was a risk that, for the good of the club, I had to take. Paul understood. He retired on doctors' orders."

In *Instant Replay*, Jerry Kramer recalls going to the Packers' offices during the off-season and finding Lombardi at his desk with his head down. "I just stood there, and Lombardi started to speak, and he opened his mouth, and still he didn't say anything. I could see he was upset, really shaken. 'What is it, Coach?' I asked. He managed to say 'I had to put Paul . . .' He was almost stuttering. 'I had to put Paul on that list, and they took him. This is a helluva business, mister, isn't it?' he asked."

There had been real love between the two. "It was in nineteen sixty-four," Lombardi remembered once, "right before a big game with the Bears, and I walked into a restaurant in Chicago and found Paul and his date at the bar. We have a rule on the Packers that if our players are going to imbibe in a public place, they must do it in moderation and at a table, and never on the eve of a game.

"When I saw him at the bar, the safety valve blew and I

shouted him out of the restaurant. The next morning, when I fined him five hundred dollars, he never even mentioned that all he was drinking was ginger ale. I know it was ginger ale because, after he left, I tasted it.

"Paul was the epitome of what you try to make every one of your players—a true believer. If we were going to play Detroit, and he knew I was worried, he'd say: 'Coach, what are you worrying about? We've got this game in the bag.' "

After Hornung retired, he talked about how strong Lombardi's hold on him was. "I had a dream the other night," he said, "that I came by and sneaked Max out after hours. Vinnie found out about it, and darned if he didn't fine me five thousand bucks, even if I wasn't with the team any longer. The thing that woke me up was that I dreamed I had paid the fine."

Paul was one of the last people to visit Vince in the hospital when the end came, and he had made weekly visits to see his coach. Before the illness struck, Paul and McGee visited Lombardi and his wife in Washington.

"It was a Saturday night," Paul recalled. "We had dinner in a good Italian restaurant with Vince and Marie, and afterward he invited us back to his house for a nightcap. Max looked at his watch and I looked at mine. It was almost eleven o'clock. Max spoke first. 'Thanks a lot, Coach, but we've got to go meet some . . . ah . . . people in a little while.'

"Vince flashed us that grin of his. 'You guys haven't changed at all,' he said. 'Every senator in this town, every congressman, and half the President's cabinet would give anything to spend time with me, and you guys are still running out on me at eleven o'clock.' He was laughing, and so were we. I really loved that man."

But Paul was gone, and Taylor was next. Jim had played out his option during the 1966 season, having failed to agree on contract terms. Taylor, in the back of his mind, thought of finishing out his playing career on home turf, and with New Orleans in the league, he had the opportunity. The former all-

America from Louisiana State lived just down the road from New Orleans, in Metarie.

During the season, when a newspaperman asked Lombardi about such a possibility, he answered, "No comment." When asked if it wouldn't be nice for Taylor to play for the Saints, before his hometown fans, he snapped: "Who the hell would block for him?"

He resented the move, because it was not his picture of loyalty. "It's his privilege," Lombardi said. "But I don't have to like it, do I?"

"I hope he comes back," Lombardi said, when May 1 had come and gone and had made Taylor a free agent. "You don't replace a Jimmy Taylor easily. I don't know if we're too far apart on money, because he hasn't told me what he wants. Taylor is a great football player. But I do think Jim Grabowski is ready to be a starting fullback, and he will be, if Taylor leaves us."

Taylor did leave, and the commissioner's office instructed the Saints to trade their number-one draft pick to Green Bay as compensation. That pick turned out to be Fred Carr, who is today one of the finest corner linebackers in the game.

"It will be difficult to win without him," Lombardi said, "but it will not be impossible. One man can't be bigger than the team."

One man wasn't.

In 1967, the NFL juggled its teams, erased the two conferences, and came up with four divisions, two to a conference. They called them the Capitol and Century, in the East, and the Coastal and Central, in the West. Green Bay was in the Central Division, along with Chicago, Detroit, and Minnesota. Because of the violence of defense as played by those four clubs, it became known as the "Black and Blue Division."

But four divisions meant nothing to Lombardi. There still were fourteen games to play, and by winning all of them—or, at worst, enough of them—he'd have another championship.

In 1967, without Jim Taylor, without Paul Hornung, the Green Bay Packers finished 9–4–1. They won their divisional championship.

The season was stellar for several of the Packers, but for none more than a rookie named Travis Williams, who ignited the league with his kickoff returns. Williams led the NFL, with eighteen of them for 739 yards, an unbelievable 41.1-yard average. And he set a record by returning four kickoffs for touchdowns. He also gained 188 yards in thirty-five rushing plays, caught five passes for 80 yards and justified his fourth-round selection out of Arizona State. Grabowski gained 466 yards in 120 carries, Anderson 402 in ninety-seven carries. Donny also caught twenty-two passes for 331 yards, but Dale led the team in receiving with thirty-five for 738 yards and five touchdowns. Jeter had eight interceptions, Wood four, and Adderley ten, combining to lead all other teams in the league.

Starr completed 115 of 210 passes for 1,823 yards and nine touchdowns. In all, it was a sound effort by a sound team. It was perhaps growing older, but it was still fired by the oratory and example of Coach Lombardi.

"When he says 'sit down,' I don't even bother to look for a chair," said Henry Jordan. It was to be Jordan's final season, and he remembers Lombardi as having been even more stern, driving the team even harder. "He sure wanted that third straight championship," Henry says. "He said he deserved it, that we did, but I think he really felt it was supposed to be his. Who was I to argue with him? I assured him we'd go out and get it."

Because of the four-division setup, the Packers had first to get past the winner of the Western Conference's other division, a devastating Los Angeles Rams team. They had flashed through their season with an 11–1–2 record, tying the Baltimore Colts but being awarded the title because they beat Baltimore twice. They were to play the Packers in Milwaukee, Green Bay's home-away-from-home stadium.

The Green Bay residents were unperturbed, never fearing a Rams victory, which would have denied them a chance to see a postseason game. "It will be cold in Milwaukee," said a local pharmacist. "The Packers know how to play in cold. What do beach boys know?"

That game turned out to be the Chuck Mercein revival. Chuck Mercein? You might remember him as a fullback for Yale. He kicked field goals, too, and the New York Giants drafted him. But Chuck couldn't kick the big-league field goals, and he wasn't fast enough. So, finally, he was waived. It was 1967, and Washington picked him up. But the Redskins' head coach, Otto Graham, decided not to activate Mercein immediately. He dispatched him to the taxi squad, the ready reserves.

Meanwhile, Green Bay was grinding out another championship season when disaster struck. Vince Lombardi's running backs staggered and were injured, dwindled and diminished. Ben Wilson was hurt. Elijah Pitts had a bad knee. Donny Anderson suffered bruises. Grabowski hurt his thigh. Almost any running back would do.

Lombardi heard about Mercein through his friend Wellington Mara, whom he had telephoned seeking other men. Vince reached Mercein by telephone at a temporary residence in Washington, D.C.

"Have you signed with the Redskins yet?" he asked.

"Who is this?" Mercein countered.

"Vince Lombardi," said Vince Lombardi.

"No, sir, I haven't. When do you want me there?" asked Chuck Mercein.

Suddenly, after the eighth game of the season, Chuck was a Packer. He looked leaner and meaner in that green-and-gold uniform. He seemed to hit holes quicker than he ever had for the Giants, and he was a stronger blocker.

"When you play for Mister Lombardi you do all the things

he tells you to do," Chuck smiled to a visitor. "You are ter-rified not to do as he says."

It was December 23, 1967. Los Angeles took an early 7–0 lead, but Green Bay won it, 28–7. Chuck Mercein scored a 6-yard touchdown that put the game out of reach. He carried the ball a dozen times. He caught two passes. He helped catapult the Packers into a rematch with Dallas for the NFL championship.

Yes, Dallas. Lombardi had been right about the future of the Cowboys. They were 9–5, having won the Capitol Division with ease, since Philadelphia, at 6–7–1, was the runner-up.

Dallas had its stars back, and the Cowboys had their minds made up that this time, this year, it would come out differently. "I am sick and tired of taking second best to Vince Lombardi," the dour Tom Landry growled at his team. "I won't have it anymore."

It was December 31, and Green Bay was frozen in. The morning of the game dawned to the noise of shattering windows. The temperature was thirteen degrees below zero. There were thirty-mile-an-hour winds. If you care about wind-chill factors, that made it equivalent to forty-eight below zero.

Walking outside was an effort, for the chill hit you smack in the face and drove you back for cover. Ears were painfully frostbitten, fingers didn't stand a chance, and feet wrapped in three pairs of wool socks were numb in minutes.

The game came to be known as the Zero Bowl. "I remember putting down a paper cup of coffee on the TV booth counter," said Frank Gifford, who was in broadcasting by then. "A few minutes later I picked it up, and it had frozen solid."

The Cowboys were stunned. No one ever remembered weather this cold. This was not football weather. "It's as cold for them as it is for you," Landry pleaded, but he knew it was not.

Dallas played gallantly. A 50-yard option pass from Danny

Reeves to Lance Rentzel gave the Cowboys a 17–14 lead, and that's how it stood going into the fourth quarter. It was late, late in the game when Green Bay received a punt to put the ball in play at its own 34-yard line.

On second and 4, Mercein took a handoff from Starr and half-skated, half-sliced his way to the 45, a 7-yard gain. First down. The Packers moved into Cowboy territory as the home fans cheered in frozen ecstasy. On a third-and-7 play, Starr chucked to Donny Anderson, who gained 9 to the 30. First down.

Now Bart went for a sideline pass, figuring the corner linebacker for the Cowboys, Chuck Howley, would have to brake too suddenly on a fast-slickening field. He was right. Mercein beat his man, broke a tackle, and moved 19 yards to the Dallas 11. Again, first down.

Now Starr went back to Mercein, on a simple off-tackle slant. Chuck turned it into 8 gigantic yards, moving to the Cowboys' 3. Anderson got the first down on the one, and two plays later—with 13 seconds to go—it was Starr's date with destiny.

"It was a dumb call," Landry would say much later. "They had time for maybe two plays, passes, and then a field goal to tie it. If Bart didn't get across on his play, the clock would have run out. We would have made it run out."

Starr had gone to the sideline to get instructions from Lombardi—it really was Lombardi's call. This was the Packers last time out, and the obvious call was a field goal. There would be no time to recoup if a run failed.

Don Horn, a reserve quarterback, listened in on the conference. "Coach Lombardi gave Starr a choice of two running plays," he said. "He didn't even discuss a field goal. I guess he figured Dallas wouldn't expect him to run. So he ran."

Starr went back to the huddle. He called for a quarterback sneak over Kramer, the right guard. And he gave his command with more than the usual authority.

"Dammit," he screamed, "I want it in there, nothing short of the goal. It's up to you, Kramer."

"That," smiles Kramer, "was the first time all season Bart had used a cuss word. I was so shocked I said 'yes, sir.'"

So Kramer drove into Jethro Pugh and Bob Lilly, and hit them low and hard. His feet began to slip on the icy muck, but he drove with his body. Starr followed him in, pushing against his rump. And when the tower of bodies fell, Starr was a foot inside the end zone. Touchdown. Final score: Green Bay 21, Dallas 17.

It was Green Bay weather, and it was the Green Bay field, but it wasn't until 13 seconds remained that it became Green Bay's game.

The Super Bowl was next, this time in sunny Miami, and the opposition was to come from the Oakland Raiders, who had steamrollered Houston, 40–7, for the AFL championship.

"Sure I think we'll win," Don Horn said a few days before the game. "This team always has a feeling of quiet confidence before a big game. Playing with the Packers is nothing short of sensational. There's a special feeling on this team; it's like having thirty-nine fraternity brothers. The Packers win because we're afraid of *him*. Tough isn't the word for Lombardi, because it's inadequate. The veterans fear him even more than the rookies because they know what he can do. Lombardi demands respect at home, on the field, and in the community. It's the same in a restaurant as on the field. I really don't know how he does it, but I've thought about it a lot. If I ever figure it out, I'm going to retire and write a book. The first thing to understand is that you adjust yourself to the idea that Lombardi is the complete authority. His way is the right way."

"We make few rules," was a Lombardi phrase. "Those we make, we keep."

Super Bowl II was played on January 14, 1968. The temperature in the Orange Bowl was sixty-eight. The wind was from the west, at a balmy fourteen miles per hour. It was as far removed from the misery of the NFL title game as the mind can imagine.

Oakland was a solid team. It had run roughshod through the AFL with a 13–1 record, having scored 468 points and given up just 233. Green Bay had scored only 332, surrendered 209.

The Raiders were led by AFL's passing champion, Daryle Lamonica. The runners were Pete Banaszak and Hewritt Dixon. For receivers, Lamonica had Bill Miller, Fred Biletnikoff, Billy Cannon, and Warren Wells. Protecting him in exemplary fashion were such men as Walt Svihus, Gene Upshaw, Jim Otto, Harry Schuh, and Wayne Hawkins.

Defensively, the Raiders were terrors. The front was made up of Ben Davidson (6 feet 7 inches, 285 pounds), Ike Lassiter, Tom Keating, and Dan Birdwell. The three linebackers were Gus Otto in the middle and Dan Connors and Bill Laskey.

Willie Brown and Kent McCloughan, perhaps two of the finest cornerbacks in the AFL, were starters in the secondary, along with the safeties Dave Grayson and Rodger Bird.

It never mattered to the proud Packers.

Chandler started things with the first of four field goals, making it 3–0 in the first quarter. It was a 39-yard boot. Then he added one of 20 yards in the second period, while Starr threw a 62-yard strike to Dowler, building Green Bay's lead to 13–0.

Oakland countered with a 23-yard pass from Lamonica to Miller, then sat back hypnotized as Chandler kicked his third, from the 43, Anderson scored from the 2, Chandler made it four for four from the 31, and Adderley returned an interception 60 yards. With 3:57 elapsed in the last quarter, the score was 33–7. When Oakland struck for its second touchdown, on another 23-yard pass to Miller, it mattered little.

Ben Wilson had gained 65 yards on the ground, Anderson 48, Grabowski 36. Starr made thirteen of twenty-four passes for 202 yards. Dowler caught two passes for 71 yards, Dale four for 43, Marv Fleming four for 35, Anderson two for 18. Even old Max McGee caught one for 35 yards. Lamonica was hounded ceaselessly, getting dropped three times while completing just fifteen of thirty-four attempts. The Packers held advantages in every major category, including first downs, total yardage, and number of plays. Green Bay also recovered two Oakland fumbles while not committing one.

Lombardi was more subdued, having been roundly criticized for his harsh words about Kansas City. "I have to say we moved the ball well," he offered. "We didn't get into the end zone often enough, but we got the three-pointers every time, and that's the main thing. That's a real good football team we played today, but it's difficult to compare them to Kansas City. That was a year ago. We took away their outside running; yes, it's tough to run outside on us. They blitzed more than we expected, but I wouldn't say it surprised me. When you fall behind like that, you have to blitz. Let's say they blitzed more than they have in the past."

Billy Cannon, the Raiders' tight end, was a veteran of many seasons, and he knew about the Green Bay Packers.

"The Packers never change," he said, somewhat wistfully. "They just come at you and beat you. I thought the whole game would depend on the pass rush. We got a good pass rush, but they capitalized on every single mistake we made."

Henry Jordan was the kindest of all. "Oakland is as good as some NFL teams. The Raiders had a better-balanced attack than what we faced last year. Next year, I dare say, it'll go right down to the wire. The Raiders might have felt like we felt in nineteen sixty, when we lost to the Eagles. I haven't forgotten it yet. You can say you know how much it means, and you think you are ready to play your best, but maybe you're not. It's hard to realize until you've been there. The AFL is improving tremendously in execution—not in personnel, because they've had that right along. Next year they could be right up there with us."

Asked about his future, an often-mentioned retirement, Jordan joked: "I'm playing them one at a time. As Jordan goes, so go the Packers. Haven't you heard Coach Lombardi say that? Right, neither have I. One of Lombardi's secrets is the depth of his bench. No one man makes that much difference."

Jerry Kramer, much later, provided a bit of insight on this. "Coach flat out asked Fuzzy: 'When are you going to quit, Thurston?' At the time, Fuzzy was angry with him, for pushing him out that way. But in a year he came back to me and said Lombardi was right all the time. 'He made me get out on top, before I embarrassed myself,' Fuzzy said."

Thurston did retire.

And so did Vince Lombardi.

The Man in the Front Office

DURING THE TIME IN MIAMI BEFORE THE SECOND SUPER Bowl, many reports circulated that Lombardi was coaching his final game for Green Bay. It was said that he had decided to retire, to assume the single post of general manager, and that he had already informed those close to the team as well as several of the players.

A group of writers assigned to the game immediately pledged to broach this subject at the next day's interview session with Lombardi at the team's lodgings in Fort Lauderdale.

We did, four of us.

"No, I don't think I'll retire yet," Lombardi laughed, strangely subdued. "I still have a game to think about planning, and I don't have time for anything else. Don't you fellows have anything to ask about the Packers, or the Raiders? I'm not that important to this team."

He was, of course. But the neat evasions only fired our curiosity more. After the game, Lombardi skirted the issue again. "It wasn't our best effort. All year it seems like when we get a couple of touchdowns ahead we let up. Maybe that's the sign of a veteran team. I don't know. Am I going to retire? Well . . . no comment."

And he just smiled.

But several of the players suspected he had coached his last game. Kramer said that in the second half the Packers pulled themselves up and drove harder and harder into the Raiders. "Some of us old heads got together," Kramer recalled. "We decided we'd play the last thirty minutes for the old man. I wouldn't be surprised if Lombardi retired before too long, and all of us love him. We didn't want to let him down."

Lombardi's pregame address to the team had a sentimental, almost imploring tone, as if this were, indeed, the last chance:

"It's very difficult for me to say anything. Anything I could say would be repetitious. This is our twenty-third game this year. I don't know of anything I could tell this team. Boys, I can only say this to you: You're a good football team. You are a proud football team. You are the world champions. You are the champions of the National Football League for the third time in a row, for the first time in the history of the National Football League. That's a great thing to be proud of. But let me say just this: All the glory, everything that you've had, everything that you've won, is going to be small in comparison to winning this one. This is a great thing for you. You are the only team maybe in the history of the National Football League to ever have this opportunity to win the Super Bowl twice. Boys, I tell you I'd be so proud of that I just fill up with myself. I just get bigger and bigger and bigger. It's not going to come easy. This is a club that's gonna hit you. They're gonna try to hit you, and you got to take it out of them. You got to be forty tigers out there. That's all. Just hit. Just run. Just block and tackle. If you do that, there's no question what the answer's going to be in this ball game. Keep your poise. Keep your poise. You've faced them all. There's nothing they can show you out there you haven't faced a number of times. Right?"

(AP Wirephoto)

Lombardi and his $400,000 bonus baby, Jim Grabowski, 1965.
Ray Nitschke pauses in the fray to take a few calm breaths.

(Vernon J. Biever Photo)

Chandler, in clean uniform, has just kicked ball out of the mud
in 1965 victory over Cleveland for the NFL championship.

(AP Wirephoto)

The triumphs of '66: After winning championship over Dallas.
Below, Commissioner Rozelle presents first Super Bowl trophy.

(Vernon J. Biever Photo)

Vince and Marie Lombardi in a relaxed mood. The three sere-
naders are "Fuzzy" Thurston, Paul Hornung, and Max McGee.

Zero Bowl: Starr (15) scoring on quarterback sneak with 13 seconds left. Kramer (64) led the way.

Super Bowl II: Anderson (44) rolls out, with Gale Gillingham (68), Jerry Kramer (64) blocking.

(Vernon J. Biever Photo)

Lombardi made his retirement as Packers head coach official in a February, 1968, announcement at the Oneida Golf Club.

Lombardi at 1969 Redskins training camp: Left, he bends over in disgust at one play. But at right, he applauds his players.

In February of 1968, Vince Lombardi resigned as head coach of the Green Bay Packers. He retained his position as general manager. The official announcement, made at the Oneida Golf and Riding Club in Green Bay, drew a large, somber crowd. Vince kept it brief. "Because of the nature and growth of the business and the corporate structure of the Packers, I believe it impossible for me to try and do both jobs. There aren't any owners here. I have to make all the decisions."

One of the first decisions he made was to retain his $50,000 annual salary. "I'm being adequately paid for the first time," he joked. He had earned it.

Lombardi had spent nine seasons as the head coach of the Packers—not one of them a losing season. His cumulative record was a phenomenal 89–29–3. He led his teams to two Super Bowl victories, five league championships, and six Western Conference titles.

Four times he was acclaimed as coach of the year. Counting preseason and postseason games, Lombardi's over-all Green Bay coaching record was 141–39–4, a percentage of .783. Of ten postseason games, the Packers had won nine.

But he had never been too preoccupied with football to become part of his community. Among his many activities over the nine years, he had served on the Green Bay Council for Human Relations, was president of the Wisconsin Mental Health Association, chairman of the state Cancer Fund, and director of the Pop Warner League program.

That Lombardi was a man to be reckoned with in the town of Green Bay is borne out by such stories as the one told by Emlen Tunnell, the outstanding safetyman, who played for the Giants when Vince was there. Tunnell, who still holds the NFL record for pass interceptions—seventy-nine over a fourteen-year career—later followed him to Green Bay.

"When I got to Green Bay," Tunnell said, "there wasn't a colored family in town. I really didn't have a place to live. Vince never even thought of that, because I honestly don't think he knew what color anybody was, just if they could play ball.

"But it could be a problem, sleeping in parks and stuff, and I went to him. He was kind of shocked. 'You mean you don't know where to stay?' he said. 'That's right, Coach. I don't know what to do.' Well, he called up a hotel in town, told them he needed a room for one of his best players, told them he wanted a special rate for me, and gave them my name. Then he stopped. 'Oh, yes,' he added. 'The player is a Negro. That won't make any difference to you, will it?' Only he didn't really make that a question. It was a statement. I spent many happy hours in that hotel, and I got along just great with the people. Green Bay is a great place to live."

Soon after the rumors began that Green Bay might be losing its favorite football coach, the question of who would succeed Lombardi arose. It was answered quickly, at the time he made his retirement official.

Lombardi's choice would have been Norman Van Brocklin. He had come to respect and admire the Hall of Fame quarterback during Van Brocklin's years as head coach of the Minnesota Vikings and the Atlanta Falcons. The feeling was mutual. In fact, "Dutch" Van Brocklin often admitted that he had been converted to Lombardi's style of football—simple and brutal.

"By observing him as an opposing coach?" a newsman once asked.

"No, by getting beat by him so often," Van Brocklin said. "When I was a quarterback, I tried to put points on the board on every play. He played three, four, six yards at a time. Move the ball. Get a first down. Control the game. I had to play ball control against him because the Packers would keep the ball for six or seven minutes with their offense and running plays and ball-control passes, the comebackers and turnouts. He had a great defense, complemented by a great kicking game and specialists. His teams were so strong they could blow you out of the stadium. They were well-trained and motivated. They went on the field thinking they could not be beaten. I played for him in a Pro Bowl. He kept it simple. He was very firm, but he was a sensitive man."

Lombardi had to offer the job first to Phil Bengtson, who had been with him longest of all his assistant coaches. Vince had hired him in 1958 as his defensive coach. He was capable and quietly brilliant—in fact, the brains behind the Packer defense.

"I remembered a game when the Giants played San Francisco," Lombardi once said. That was at a time when "Red" Hickey was the San Francisco head coach. "The Forty-niners' defense was very impressive. I liked the simplicity, but I knew a great deal of work and thought had gone into making anything that simple. When I found out it was Phil who was in charge of the defense, I determined to have him on my staff if and when I became a head coach."

Bengtson joined Lombardi on the Packers, and almost a decade later, when Lombardi felt obliged to offer the job to him, Bengtson accepted and became head coach. He knew that Lombardi would be sitting back there somewhere, watching, comparing, judging. The players had a sense of that also, and they were uneasy.

Anticipating just such a mood, Lombardi tried to check it before it could hurt team morale. "I am not going to interfere," he said publicly. "This is Phil's team. He will do what he thinks best. I will stick to the front office, and I will not offer advice unless I am asked. I would have taken no interference when I was coaching, and I will not ask Bengtson to live under any other guidelines. It's up to him. He has his job, and I have mine."

Lombardi's job was the business end of football, and the closest he ever got to the football end of football was making trades. Otherwise, Vince Lombardi spent his time on purchasing hot dogs for the concession stands, working with the ground crews, getting programs printed, negotiating player contracts and rookie bonuses, paying bills, writing letters, and reporting to the Packers' board of directors. It was an unlikely job for such a man.

"I don't like this at all," he said after a while. "I didn't think one man could take the pressures and responsibilities of both jobs, but I'm not sure there's enough in the one job to satisfy me. Sure I miss the game. I always will."

Bengtson, too, was having problems, and they were only in part connected with football. The Packers had developed a Vince Lombardi habit, and now they were sweating out a withdrawal.

"We missed his inspirational genius, his tactical brain," said Jerry Kramer, who retired after that 1968 season. "Nobody thought Phil Bengtson would be another Lombardi. He was a totally different sort of man, a gentler man, a calmer man. The players wanted to win for Phil, desperately. I suppose several of the guys had that feeling, a resentment that Lombardi had gotten too much credit for their efforts. I never felt that way myself; I honestly felt that Vince was the difference between a good team and a great one. In professional football, the teams are just about equal physically; all of them have players with strength and size and speed. The big difference, I think, between winning and losing is motivation, and nobody will deny that Vince motivated us. He made us hate him most of the time, but even this hatred, this half-serious suspicion that he treated us all like dogs, served to unify us. We had a single target for all our frustrations. We lost that in 1968."

Jim Weatherwax, a defensive tackle, said: "Sure, we wanted to win for Phil. But we wanted to win just to show everybody that it wasn't just Lombardi these past few years, that it wasn't all him, that we can have a good season without him."

Bengtson spent much of each week working with his defense, as usual. He let his assistants prepare the offense. The change in emphasis led to resentment and friction among the players.

The games did not go as they once had gone, and other teams saw the difference in the Packers. "They just didn't have the same fire," said the Detroit Lions tackle Alex Karras after the third game of the season, a 23-17 Detroit victory. "I even heard some guys yelling at each other, and that never happened. They seemed to have blown their cool."

The Rams beat the Packers 16–14 in the fifth game of the season, and the Los Angeles safety Ed Meador commented: "Their offense—I don't know—it just didn't seem as cohesive as it used to. There were little mistakes, just small things, but the old Packers didn't do those kinds of things. Starr was as smart as ever—he just didn't have the same kind of team spirit behind him."

The season opened with a victory. But soon it was win one, lose one, win two, lose two. And there were the Packers, 5–5–1. Surprisingly though, they were still in the Central Division race. They went to San Francisco knowing they had to win to stay in contention.

"Bengtson told us, before the game," Jerry Kramer remembers, "how much we had to gain and how much we had to lose. He talked about the past glories of the Packers. He got as emotional as we ever saw him. But it just wasn't the same."

Green Bay jumped out to a 20–14 lead, then blew it. The final score was San Francisco 27, Packers 20.

"I don't know if we would have won if Lombardi had still been coaching," Kramer said. "I tend to think that Vince, even Vince, would have had a hard time making us champions in 1968. But I really missed him for the key games. He was a genius of the locker-room speech. He always knew exactly how to treat us. In 1967, for instance, before the Bears game that clinched the divisional title, he didn't say anything but a silly little joke to break the tension. A few weeks later, before the game for the Western Conference title, he quoted passionately from one of Saint Paul's Epistles and really fired us up. He played us like a virtuoso."

The situation worsened. In one game, Willie Davis, the defensive captain, came to the sidelines steaming after the Packers had been scored on. He growled to Bengston: "Get that man out of there. What are you waiting for? That man's hurting us. Get him out of there." Davis never mentioned the man by name—it was Tom Brown, who was to rejoin Lombardi in Washington. But no one on the Packers would have let go that way with Vince prowling the sidelines.

After a loss to the Vikings, Lombardi made one of his infrequent appearances in the locker room. Many of the players were already in street clothes. He spoke softly to a few of the men, roamed around in a confused manner, and finally stalked away, grumbling: "Too damn many blue shirts in here. Too many sideburns."

Lombardi had the Green Bay press box in Lambeau Field remodeled, to include a soundproof section for himself and, just occasionally, a guest. It cost $50,000, and he insisted on the soundproofing. "You newspaper guys will never get to hear me screaming at the coach of the Packers," he said with a smile. "What I say in that part of the press box will stay there."

Midway through the season, the itch to coach became overpowering, to get down on the field again and mingle with the players. More than he had imagined, he missed the locker room and practice, the movie sessions and the preparing. During this period, he told a friend, "I think I'll always be loyal to Green Bay, but I don't have to be here to be loyal."

Lombardi was still a demigod in Green Bay. He was pursued by the most influential residents, catered to, wooed, partied. But he felt out of the mainstream, he said, not fully absorbed in doing something constructive.

"Hot dogs!" he snorted to a preseason visitor. "How the hell many ways can you buy and sell hot dogs?" And that was only August.

But Green Bay had a coach. Bengtson was working as hard as a man can work, trying to find the secret to Lombardi's success. Bengtson was the man on the spot, the man the players were hoping would find the answers. Bengtson had the job, and it was Lombardi who had given it to him. It would not be Lombardi who took it away.

"Phil is the coach of the Green Bay Packers," Lombardi said to a man who had come to question the floundering team and seek explanations. "Ask Phil. Don't ask me. I'm only the general manager."

Marie Lombardi remembers that he was "even more annoyed and upset when he got home at night than when he was coaching." Friends, too, noticed the difference. He was torn between loyalty to Bengtson and the team and his desire to re-enter the arena. He knew he could not return in Green Bay. He knew, also, that he would not return to the Giants. Mara had replaced Allie Sherman with Alex Webster, and he had not asked Vince to take the job first.

"When I asked him to replace Jim Lee," Mara says, "that was the first and last time I made such a request. I never asked Vince to take over when we dismissed Allie. I never offered him stock in the team, and I never offered him a job. It was too late then. I think both of us realized that. Who knows? If the Packers had allowed him to leave in nineteen sixty-one, and if he had become the Giants' coach, who is to say he would have had the glory he experienced as a coach? Perhaps things all worked out for the best. He was a dear friend, but I asked him only once to become my coach."

Lombardi stewed. He had expected more challenge in the front office. He had looked forward to dealing with a threatened players' strike, the mechanics of the merger with the American Football League, Packers' contracts, the college draft, negotiations of a business nature. But the strike never materialized, the merger had gone very smoothly, the players were satisfied with their financial terms, and the draft had even then become a computer's chore.

Vince tried golf. He had often played at the game, never

with much success. He and Mara, a fine handicap golfer, had amused themselves often through the years with golf stories told at Lombardi's expense. Now he had time on his hands, and the Oneida Country Club course was nearby. So he played golf. Breaking eighty-five was a goal he soon reached, but it did not hold his interest. Not did this game take his mind off the other game, his game.

Finally, almost inevitably, the rumors began. A story appeared saying that a group had offered to purchase the financially troubled Philadelphia Eagles because they had received assurances from Lombardi that he would join them.

It did not work out.

There was another story, more incongruous, that Lombardi would become the next commissioner of baseball. Football men laughed. Lombardi said nothing. It did not work out.

John Mecom, Jr., the young man who has used his oil millions to run the New Orleans Saints, offered Lombardi part ownership of the Saints. But that situation was hardly the right one for a man of Lombardi's reputation, and he quickly begged off.

Atlanta offered him a multiple-year contract as head coach and general manager with $1 million as the lure. It was tempting. The Falcons had the nucleus of a team—indeed, much more than Vince had found in Green Bay in 1958. But he did not, he said, "feel it." And so that proposal, too, was shunted aside. The Falcons hired Norm Van Brocklin.

The Boston Patriots—now the New England Patriots— made an ownership proposal to Lombardi, if he would coach as well. He turned that down. But it must have been gratifying to a man of such pride to know that he was so much in demand.

It was rumored that the New York Jets were interested in Lombardi's services. This was one idea he found particularly attractive. The Jets' organization had just gone through a shake-up, in which three members of the group that had purchased the bankrupt franchise from the AFL now bought out the shares held by David A. Werblin, president of the organization. There had been bad blood there. Philip Iselin, who followed as president, had been one of those who resented "Sonny" Werblin's great influence with the team, specifically with its star quarterback, Joe Willie Namath. Werblin had offered to buy out the three partners—Iselin, Townsend Martin, and Leon Hess—or to let them buy up his shares at current market value. They bought.

Lombardi was impressed by Namath's raw talent, as were most football people, and he was convinced he could straighten out the rambunctious, carefree Joe Willie. Namath was as far removed from Bart Starr as football from baseball, and the challenge of Namath tickled Lombardi's fancy.

But no. Weeb Ewbank, the Jets' head coach and general manager, let it be known that he did not choose to retire. Iselin backed off. He would back off again later that season, when a group headed by Allie Sherman made overtures toward buying the franchise. The deal was said to be "ninety-five percent done" when Iselin dallied so long over minor issues that the Sherman group walked out entirely.

Politics, too, beckoned Vince Lombardi. He was a hero in Wisconsin, and both parties wooed him to accept a nomination for the governorship. He declined this, too, still hoping to do what he knew best—coach football.

Meanwhile, the Packers were stumbling their way to a 6–7–1 season, their first losing season in ten years.

Super Bowl time of 1969 provided the setting for a fateful meeting over breakfast between Vince Lombardi and Edward Bennett Williams, the renowned Washington, D.C., criminal lawyer. Williams had assumed the position of president of the Washington Redskins organization upon the confining—and ultimately mortal—illness of the team's founder, George Preston Marshall.

Williams is an imposing man, incisive and determined. In football, his goal was perfection. He had been successful in luring away Otto Graham, the Cleveland Browns' Hall of Fame quarterback, from a secure position as athletic director and head coach of the United States Coast Guard Academy in New London, Connecticut. But Graham had not worked the wonders expected of him in the three years he held the job. After a quick start, the Redskins had become another run-of-the-mill club, and the three-year record was 17–22–3. Perhaps the most memorable game in Graham's career with the Redskins was a 72–41 victory over the Giants in 1966, a game in which he called for a field-goal attempt with nine seconds to play and his team ahead, 69–41.

Otto made few friends. He said what was on his mind—whether he should have or not—and he ruled the Redskins with a curious mixture of laissez-faire and autonomy. Curfews were broken, team rules were disregarded, and all the while Otto either smiled or fretted. But never did he assume total command.

The discouraged Williams commented that "what the Redskins need is a crackdown coach with a winning background." No names had been mentioned, but Edward Bennett Williams had only one name in mind—Vince Lombardi. He approached Lombardi discreetly, and they talked in a general way.

Wellington Mara says Lombardi told him in November, 1968, about a Redskins offer, which involved part ownership. "I did not offer advice, nor did he ask for any," Mara remembers. "It was simply a case of one friend telling another something important but confidential. I was happy for him, if he wanted coaching. It seemed like a fine arrangement."

Then came the Super Bowl breakfast, and after that things moved quickly. In the middle of January the NFL held its college-player draft. Graham was there for the Redskins, but the rumors had reached him. "I think I'll call Lombardi," said Graham to his staff. "I'll ask him if he wants to trade Donny Anderson and Jim Grabowski for A. D. Whitfield." Whitfield was an obscure Redskins' running back. "If he says yes, I might as well go home."

The draft done, Graham packed up and went to California on an extended golfing holiday. He was not to return as the coach of any team, but he was one of the last to learn officially of his fate.

Washington newspapers proclaimed the news on February 1 that Redskins' stock transfers had been arranged to let Lombardi buy into the club. Two days later, the same newspaper announced Graham's ouster. The next day, Green Bay's president, Dominick Olejniczak, asked for time until the entire forty-five man board of directors could vote on Lombardi's request for release from his contract. Many of the members of the board were upset. Several accused Lombardi of being disloyal. But none was able to muster enough voting strength to block the release.

On the sixth of February, Lombardi arrived for a press conference in the nation's capital. In the Sheraton-Carlton Hotel's Chandelier Room, he was introduced as the new general manager, head coach, and part owner—with five percent —of the Washington Redskins. "In spite of what you've heard," he told the assemblage, "I can't walk on water. Not even when the Potomac is frozen."

Vince spoke of the chance to own a piece of the team as what finally moved him to leave Green Bay. "Every man wants to own something," he said. "Creating, not maintaining, is the ultimate challenge."

"Somehow," said a resident of Green Bay, "I feel he's cheating us. We had him before anyone knew his name. He gave us our name. He gave us the years of glory with the Packers. I understand why he wants to leave, but I don't know if I can forgive him for doing it. He belongs to Green Bay. This is where he should stay."

The town was as resentful as the Packer players had been.

Indeed, the town had been virtually an extension of the team. I remember entering the barber shop of the Northland Hotel in 1965, during that long week between the playoff and championship games. It was nearly four o'clock in the afternoon.

"I'm sorry," said the barber. "But we're ready to close up."

Just then Vince strode in, occupied a chair, and waited. The barber scurried over to cut his hair. Lombardi looked at me and back at the barber. Then he looked directly at the second barber, who was in a chair.

"Cut his hair," Lombardi said, pointing at me with his chin.

"Yes, sir, Coach," the barber said. "Right this way, sir."

Just as he had once taken his last leave of his Packers, so now he was putting the town of Green Bay behind him. What must that final day in Green Bay have been like?

Lambeau Field is on Lombardi Avenue, and you drive past it—in fact, you turn left at the corner—on the way to Austin Straubel Airport. Did Vince glance at the stadium on his last drive out of town? Did he hear the crowds, the official's whistle, the crash of shoulder pads, the thunk of a punt? Did he remember the games? Did he think of the Zero Bowl, with Starr's last-second sneak? Did he think of the exultant 37–0 slaughter of the Giants? Did he see in his mind the players who wore the green and gold? Did he picture them on the field, blocking and tackling, running and leaping, laughing, crying, fighting? Which player sprang first to his mind? Was it Hornung? Starr? Kramer? Dale?

The ride out of town must have moved Vince Lombardi, who was an emotional man, as much as it moved Green Bay. It would not be forgotten—or forgiven. It was an end.

But it was also a beginning for Vince Lombardi. He had a team again, not a good team, not a winner, but a team with talent and potential.

Having known Lombardi, I think that is the thought he held in his mind. He had work to do, games to win, men to mold.

Lombardi Goes to
Washington

TWO MEN, A GRIZZLED VETERAN AND AN APPLE-GREEN
rookie, stand as tributes to Vince Lombardi in his one brief
season with the Washington Redskins.

Christian Adolph Jurgensen was the veteran. Some call him
Sonny; some call him Jurgy. All call him the finest quarterback in professional football, bar none. "He is," says a scout
for the New York Giants, "the greatest pure passer in the
game. If Sonny is hot, no defense has a chance to stop him.
He's one of the few men who can lift an ordinary team to the
top through his performance alone."

Sonny Jurgensen is also a fast and fancy off-the-field gad-
about. And Sonny has an unbecoming pot belly. He has had it
every year he has played in the NFL except for one—the 1969
season. He had it back in the 1970 season. Vince Lombardi
made him work it off in 1969.

"I learned to love that man," Jurgy says. "I also learned
more in my first five days of listening to him than I did in

twelve years of listening to other coaches. I envy all those guys from Green Bay. They had Vince for nine years. We only had him for one, just long enough for him to educate us as to what it takes to be a winner."

Larry Brown, thirteen years Jurgensen's junior, was the rookie, a running back, too small, too light, deaf in one ear. He had been an eighth-round draft choice, unheralded, never seen by most of the scouts.

"I was a little uptight about playing for Lombardi," Brown says. "When the Redskins drafted me, he wasn't the coach. I didn't know what to expect. All I knew about him was what I read in the papers and watched on television. I knew he was tough, but I knew he was a winner. I had heard he was impossible to like and difficult to understand. That's what I thought I knew. Know something? I didn't know anything at all.

"Coach Lombardi was a teacher, the best I ever saw. But not just football. Coach Lombardi taught me to be a man, to be proud of what I am. He also taught me the wisdom of hard work and dedication, and he proved to me that if you are better prepared and more determined than the next man, you will come out ahead of him.

"Even if he is more talented, it will still hold true. Coach changed my whole life. I loved him."

Brown showed up July 10, 1969, at the Redskins' summer training camp in Carlisle, Pennsylvania. "I was scared to death," he says, "just looking at him."

So were the rest of the Redskins, veterans and rookies alike. "The idea of playing for Vince Lombardi," said the offensive tackle Jim Snowden, "frightens me."

Soon the players knew what it had been like in Green Bay. "I don't think we stopped working from the day camp opened until the day the season ended," said Jurgy, "and the man made us love it. I mean, I had never been much for all those exercises and calisthenics and drills and such, but he looked

for me to be the team leader"—Lombardi always considered
that part of the quarterback's duties—"and I just had to do it
all. I got to like it. The man was super."

Lombardi had gathered around him a talented staff. Bill
Austin and Lew Carpenter had been with him in Green Bay.
Austin would follow him as coach of the Redskins. He also
hired Harland Svare, once an all-pro linebacker with the
Giants, whom he had grown to respect during the New York
years, Don Doll, George Dickson, and Mike McCormack.

The task was simple, in Lombardi's mind. He had to build
a winner out of this ragtag collection of Redskins. The season
before, Washington's record had been 5–9, a dismal performance despite the presence of such individuals as Jurgy,
Charley Taylor, Bobby Mitchell, Jerry Smith, Sam Huff, and
Pat Fischer. There was no organization, there was no discipline, and there was very little team pride. "It was a job of
work," said Huff. "We played because it said we had to in our
contracts. I had never been accustomed to that kind of system.
In New York, the Giants were always together as a team."

Lombardi studied films all that winter, getting ready to open
camp. He found the situation intolerable. "I don't know what
I could have been thinking to come here," he said to Austin
one day, disconsolate. "This is just awful. Why the hell did I
ever come back to this?"

But he worked even harder when he became morose. It
must have seemed like the beginning in Green Bay all over
again, and he knew what he had accomplished there. "I am
not going to come here to coach a losing team," he had told
the press on the day of his official hiring. "The Redskins will
be winners this year." The reporters had snickered. The Redskins had a history of losing that seemed far too powerful for
one man to change. They always played well on offense, because of people like Jurgensen, throwing the ball to people like
Taylor and Mitchell and Smith. But then the defense would

take the field, and it would give everything back. The scores were silly. Jurgy would put 37 points on the scoreboard, and Cleveland would win, 42–37. Jurgy would score 35 points for the Redskins, and the Eeagles would earn a 35–35 tie. Jurgy would see to it that the Redskins scored 24 points against Philadelphia, and the Eagles would get 35. Even in victory, no lead was safe. The winning scores—38–28, 38–34, 31–28, 34–31—only served to underline the hopelessness of the Washington defense.

"The defense here is terrible," Lombardi said in March.

"I don't see how this defense ever managed to hold anybody," Lombardi said in April.

"We will have to devote all our time to building this defense," he said in May. "It is frightening to me that I might have to open a season with this unit."

By June, he had already made some moves. From the Packers he acquired Tom Brown for the tight safety position, the same Tom Brown who had played so well for him in Green Bay, and the same Tom Brown who had incurred the wrath of Willie Davis when Bengtson took over.

He brought in Dave Long, a hulking defensive end, from New Orleans. He lured Huff out of a year's retirement, telling him he must play to save the Redskins. Sam, at age thirty-five, would play admirably.

Lombardi found gems among the free agents and rookies who reported to camp. He convinced a free agent named John Hoffman that defense was fun, and Hoffman, a 6-foot 7-inch 260-pounder from the University of Hawaii, became a first-stringer. He signed Mike Bass, a cornerback, as a free agent. Bass would start, and do well.

John Didion, who had been drafted as a center, was converted to middle linebacker, the heir apparent to Huff's position the next season. "When the kid can do it," Vince told Huff, "you'll be a coach again." Harold McLinton was a sixth-round draft pick as a linebacker out of Southern University, and he, too, danced to Lombardi's tune. Slowly, excruciatingly, the Redskins made progress.

Jurgensen tells what that progress meant for him: "He called me into his office during the winter. He told me we had to talk. I sat down, and he looked at me, and he said he had heard plenty of stories about me, and he was sure I had heard plenty of stories about him. Then he said he didn't care what I had been doing, how I had been living. All he cared about was from now on. He told me I would have to be the leader, the example. He told me what he felt about the theory of quarterbacking, what his philosophy of offense was, how he felt I should play the game.

"I don't mind saying it was different than what I had been used to hearing. He tried to show me the value of the short, safe passes instead of the bombs. He said Starr became a complete quarterback when he realized the pass is only one part of a man's offense. I said something about the team not having had any real running threats, and he said not to worry about it. He said if I could adopt his style of offense, he'd find me the necessary running. I guess I had heard that before, from other coaches, but when he said it I believed it. I really believed."

Summer camp at Carlisle, Pennsylvania, started on July 10. That night, Lombardi delivered his opening address to the assembled squad.

"Gentlemen," he said, "I have never been with a loser, and I do not think I'm ready to start at this time in my career. You are here to play the game of football, and I am here to see that you play it as well as your abilities will allow. That is going to call for total dedication, which I want from every man on this team. It means dedication to himself, to the team, and to winning. Winning, gentlemen, gets to be habitual. If you can shrug off a loss, you can't be a winner. The harder you work for something, the harder it is to lose. I am going to push you and push you and push you because I get paid to win and so do you. Football is a violent game. To play you have to be tough, physically and mentally. Pride, too, because when two equal teams meet, it's the one that has pride that wins. Gentlemen, let's be winners."

Camp was torture. Under Otto Graham, the Redskins had been content to play at their conditioning, to get there at their leisure. Under Vince, they had to work to survive, not just to approach physical shape. Injuries were hidden from him. "What do you mean, it hurts?" he would shriek. "It doesn't hurt. Hurt is in the mind. Get back out there."

Under the heat of the July and August sun, players wilted and stumbled. Those who did were cut. Those who did not acquired Lombardi conditioning. "I do not ever remember working that hard," said Huff. "Not with the Giants, not with any team. But many of us discovered new things about ourselves."

What kind of things?

"Well, fatigue, for instance. If you work yourself into fatigue, to a point of thinking you are not capable of lifting a hand, of taking another step, you are wrong. He would scream and shout and implore and we'd keep going, keep moving, keep working. And then we'd find that extra reserve, somewhere, and we'd work harder. If you can get used to that, you build up your stamina. But it's hell, and you can't know how it is unless you've gone through it. I got to hate the sun. I used to root for rain. No, rain didn't mean no practice, but it meant less heat."

Lombardi scanned the waiver lists every night, and players were claimed from other teams for the standard $100 fee. Most of them never stuck, but Lombardi had to find help. He had to build the team, and he had only months to do it. The season was opening soon.

Those sportswriters who regularly cover the Redskins were astonished at the way the camp was run. "I never saw guys that tired," recalled Dave Brady, of *The Washington Post*. "They'd crawl out of bed in the morning, get to the cafeteria in time for breakfast, and then spend the rest of the day going at full speed. I had covered a lot of the Packers' games when Vince coached there, but I never saw them in summer camp. That's where he made them special. When they first showed up, they were just like everybody else. Then he built them up. By the time the season began, they were stronger and faster and quicker and more disciplined. They were tougher. Yes, tougher, mentally and physically."

Lombardi drove himself as hard as the players. He was there at eight o'clock for daily breakfast—after working for two hours on playbooks and depth charts. He was with them all day, out there in the sun, a long-billed sun visor on his head, in shirtsleeves and cleats. Moving, running, yelling, flitting from unit to unit. He was an ever-present specter of fear.

"You won't get any better unless you work at it," he told the team one night. "If you think you've worked until now, get ready to really work from now on."

It frightened them. They did not know how much more they could take of Lombardi conditioning.

In *Coach: A Season with Lombardi*, Tom Dowling has written a journal of what 1969 was like for the Redskins. The book describes the summer-camp period through the eyes of someone who is not used to seeing men tortured.

"A man fell on the practice field," he wrote, "and Lombardi screamed at him. 'Get up, get up, you can't die out there.' A writer standing nearby said: 'Why not? Why can't he die? It's a man's privilege.' "

Several players contemplated walking away from it all, going home, to normalcy, to sanity. But they stayed anyway, because—if nothing else—there was always the lure of money. All players who had been associated with Lombardi in the past had made money, gobs of money. It is as much a motivator in professional sports as pride or team spirit. For most professional athletes and especially for those who come out of the black ghettos, the money in pro football can mean lifetime security.

They stayed, and slowly the team took shape. There had been eighty-two assorted veterans and rookies who reported to Carlisle on July 10, and only thirty-two of them were to survive through the season. Eight more would join the team after the camp was disbanded.

Out of that camp, six rookies made the final squad—the place-kicker Curt Knight, the cornerback Ted Vactor, Larry Brown, John Didion, Harold McLinton, and John Hoffman. The extent of the juggling Lombardi had done with the veterans resulted in another dozen "new men" with previous NFL experience—Frank Ryan, quarterback; Bob Wade, safety; the running back Charley Harraway; Henry Dyer, fullback; Dave Kopay, halfback; the defensive back Mike Bass; the guards Dan Grimm and Steve Duich; Sam Huff; the wide receiver Bob Long; Jim Norton, defensive tackle; and the defensive end Leo Carroll.

Lombardi cut men, lopped athletes off his squad, almost fitfully. A defensive back named Aaron Martin missed a tackle in a squad game and then lay on the turf, content to have made the try. "You've got to tackle, and you've got to keep going," Vince yelled. "If you quit on me here, you'll quit on me in the games." Martin was waived.

Larry Brown emerged as a startlingly talented runner. He had been drafted out of Kansas State, a 5-foot 11-inch, 195-pound halfback who had led the Wildcats in rushing yardage for two seasons. Before that, he was the star of the team at Dodge City Junior College, also in Kansas. He was a *player,* as Lombardi defined that word. He did not complain. He did not flinch from work. He played hurt, if he had to, and he was constantly playing to that 100 percent capacity Lombardi sought.

Lombardi made a discovery about Brown later that season —that he was partly deaf in one ear. It came about when Lombardi and his staff found that Brown was slower off the ball on one side of the quarterback than on the other. So Vince had a hearing aid made and fitted to Brown's helmet. It worked marvelously.

Brown and Harraway, picked up from the Cleveland Browns, were the starting runners. Jurgensen, of course, was the quarterback. Charley Taylor and Walt Roberts were the wide receivers, Jerry Smith the tight end. Walt Rock and Jim Snowden were the tackles, Vince Promuto and Ray Schoenke the guards, Len Hauss the center.

Lombardi's defense found Hoffman and Carl Kammerer at the ends, Frank Bosch and Joe Rutgens at tackles. Huff was in the middle linebacker position, with Chris Hanburger and Tom Roussel the outside linebackers.

The secondary, which underwent constant re-evaluation, mainly consisted of Brig Owens and Rickie Harris at safeties, with Pat Fischer and Mike Bass at the corners, although Ted Vactor and Bob Wade played some.

The opening game and the two that followed were road games because the baseball season was not yet over, and the Washington Senators were using RFK Stadium.

Lombardi's first game as the head of the Redskins was played in New Orleans, and the Saints fell, 26–20. Next came the Browns, a talented, far superior team, but they didn't prove it until late in the game, when Bill Nelsen completed a crucial third-down pass to Reece Morrison on the Redskins' 15. Seconds later—with little more than a minute left—he threw for a touchdown to Garry Collins.

Lombardi was uncontrollable. "We needed one big play, and we couldn't get it," he raged. "One big play. Just one guy to knock down the quarterback. What the hell have we been trying to do all summer, if not to tell you people that big plays win games and that teams with the proper dedication make the big plays? I'm ashamed."

The Redskins fought back. After a 17–17 tie with San

Francisco in the third game of the season, they beat the Saint Louis Cardinals, 33–17, before a capacity crowd at RFK. Then came the Giants' game, also at home. Lombardi always liked to beat the Giants. This time it was an especially big game because a victory over the Giants would tell the world: *Vince Lombardi has arrived in Washington.*

Allie Sherman had been dismissed nine days before the start of the season, and Vince's protégé, Alex Webster, had somewhat surprisingly been elevated from an assistant's chair to the head coaching position. It was all new to Alex, but he quickly established a rapport with the players, and they, in turn, decided to win for good old Red. They had shocked the powerful Minnesota Vikings in their opener, and took a 3–1 record to Washington. For this game, RFK Stadium was packed again.

The Redskins stumbled in the second period. New York recovered a Larry Brown fumble on the Washington 41. Fran Tarkenton, the man who infuriated Lombardi because he quarterbacked so unorthodoxly, took New York in, hitting a few quick-out passes. Then Joe Morrison broke up the middle for 11 yards and scored. It had taken six plays, and the Giants led, 7–0.

Now Jurgensen moved the Redskins to their 42 and decided to risk it all on one play. He sent Charley Taylor down and deep, and the extraordinary wide receiver beat his man by 20 yards. It was a picture play. He was running in full stride, the green of the grass glinting back at the red and gold of his uniform. Jurgensen lofted a perfect pass of about 40 yards, a classic spiral, on the money. Taylor reached up his hands, never breaking stride, and as he neared the New York 15, the ball came to him. And it went right through his outstretched palms.

He kept running—as one wag in the press box put it, "out of fear"—and came to a stop in the end zone, gazing balefully at the ball, which was lying near the 10-yard line. The half ended with the Giants still ahead, 7–0. Lombardi stalked off the field in a black fury. Taylor was seen shaking his head, gazing at his hands and, almost fearfully, sneaking quick glances behind him at the Coach.

Whatever he said to them at halftime inspired those Redskins. No one recalls exactly what happened in the dressing room, but it is a safe assumption that no one told any Italian jokes. "Garbage," Lombardi is said to have yelled. "You men are playing garbage football. You don't deserve to wear uniforms."

They came back, and Jurgensen began moving the team well. But the Giants, who had gone through years of their own defensive problems, were now much stronger in that department. They held back the Washington assault until Tarkenton made it 14–0 with a fourteen-play, 72-yard drive—a Lombardi-type drive that consumed more than 7 minutes.

The Redskins were down by two touchdowns. The fans began to boo.

Now Washington moved. Jurgensen led a 5-minute drive, getting on the scoreboard when a furious Taylor block sprang Harraway on a 1-yard plunge. Taking the ball right back, Jurgy moved again, striking with short passes and getting running brilliance from Brown. The rookie ripped off a 41-yard sprint to the New York 24, and the score became 14–14 three plays later, when Harraway scored again.

The crowd had long since forgotten to boo, and now began to yell ceaselessly. The din reminded some in the press box of the crowds in Green Bay, years before. Lombardi could electrify fans, too. They hoped for a repeat of what he had done before.

Now the Washington safety Rickie Harris took an Ernie Koy punt on his 14 and began picking his way through the suicidal traffic of the special teams. Suddenly, near midfield, he got the one block he needed. He broke into the clear, and he was gone.

Everyone knew it, long before he crossed the goal line, and Lombardi was seen jumping up and down near the bench, his clipboard on the ground, his fists in the air.

Then disaster. Curt Knight missed the extra point. The score showed the Redskins on top by 20–14. The Giants could win it with a touchdown and the conversion. Lombardi stormed about on the sideline, yelling at no one in particular: "How could he have missed it? How? Dammit, how?"

The Giants went to work with a doggedness that would have pleased Lombardi in any other circumstances. Tarkenton was a dervish, passing here, running there, handing off, mixing his calls, and sweeping the Giants downfield.

New York started from its 32. Tarkenton hit Homer Jones for 17 yards, igniting a march. Four more first downs, nine plays, and suddenly the Giants were sitting on the Washington 9, with plenty of time to carry it off.

Morrison took the ball to the 3 before he ran into his old teammate Huff. He got no more. Still, it was dire.

And now the will of Lombardi showed itself. The Redskins, perhaps for the first time in a decade, found out about themselves, tapped hitherto unknown reserves of courage and quality.

John Fuqua tried the middle on second down, and got nothing. It was third down. Tarkenton attempted to pass to his tight end Freeman White, but Brig Owens knocked the ball down. With the crowd deafening, Tarkenton was faced with a fourth-down call. He had to try for it, since a field goal would mean less than nothing. The Giants could not be sure of getting the ball back. It had to be now.

Tarkenton dropped back, faded as only he can, with that jitterbug step that threatens to send him scampering off any second. He cocked his arm, tried to find a wide receiver, then looked for a running back. There was no clear target. The Redskin rush was getting to him. He pulled up, gazed for an instant at the confusion, and saw a gaping hole in the middle of the field. He could run it over.

He tucked the ball under his arm and dashed for the touchdown. Huff reacted. So did Pat Fischer. So did the tackle Spain Musgrove. Fischer hit him first, at the 2. Then Huff crashed down on the little quarterback, driving him back. Then Musgrove added his 270 pounds, and the Giants were dead.

It ended 20–14. The Redskins were 3–1–1.

Lombardi was thrilled with the victory, but by Tuesday he was himself again. "We played better as a team last week against the Cardinals," he said. "We were unsure of ourselves against New York. We made mistakes. We were lucky."

Sadly, the rest of the season was to turn to ashes. After the proud beginnings of that 3–1–1 start, the Redskins played the rest of the season at 4–4–1.

What had been recklessly imagined as a championship surge died aborning. The record moved to 4–1–1 with a 14–7 victory over Pittsburgh, but then the losses began—41–17 to Baltimore, 41–28 to Dallas, 24–13 to Los Angeles, 20–10 to Dallas. In the end the Redskins had scored 307 points, fifty-eight more than in the 1968 season under Graham, and had allowed 319, thirty-nine fewer than in 1968. It was the logical beginning for building a championship team.

The defense had been much stronger. And that alone helped Lombardi live up to his promise of bringing the Redskins a winning year. The over-all record was 7–5–2. And although the team had disappointed the fans' hysterical early-season hopes, it was still the first time the Redskins had won more games than they had lost in fourteen years.

Larry Brown had been the surprise. He gained 888 yards in 202 carries, fourth best in the league. He caught thirty-four passes for 302 yards. He scored four times, and he barely lost out in the rookie-of-the-year balloting to Dallas's Calvin Hill.

Jurgy had completed 62.1 percent of his passes, his best

figure in a fifteen-year career. He clicked on 274 of 442 attempts, for 3,102 yards and twenty-two touchdowns. He was splendid. He matured under Lombardi as he had not done in all of his previous seasons. He became the complete quarterback. And the six-time all-pro choice credited all of it to Lombardi.

"He told us we were going to be a team, we were going to build together. He told me I had had a good year, and he said I would have a better one next year. He taught me to react to defenses, rather than waiting for them to react to the play I had called. The man was incredible. I never learned so much, and I was never as confident of winning the following season."

Brown, who was to go on to lead the league and to top 1,000 yards gained in 1970, was overwhelmed. "I never thought a coach could help me as much as Lombardi did," he said. "I never really believed I could play NFL football, but he showed me I could if I was willing to pay the price."

Of his rookie season, Brown says: "My first year in Washington was a wonderful experience. I accomplished a lot. Being picked to play in the Pro Bowl was the peak of success, like an award. I gained a lot. Coach Lombardi was tough. Man, was he tough!

"But he treated everybody as an individual. When I came to training camp, I had no idea I would get a full chance. There were so many players. They would be there one day and gone the next. I am already setting goals for next season—to be the leading rusher again and to make the Pro Bowl team. I don't think anybody could have come into one of Lombardi's camps without reacting. I always wanted to play in a Super Bowl, and I still do. Vince Lombardi was the man who could have gotten us there. Now we'll have to do it in his memory. He was our coach, and we were his last team. That means something to me. Something special.

"Of all the things I learned from him, I guess the biggest was 'never quit.' So I run as hard when we are three touchdowns behind as I do when we are three ahead. If you pick your spots to work hard, you'll never amount to anything. It has to be a constant thing, a continuous effort. Coach Lombardi taught me that much, and I'll never forget it. The difference between winners and losers is how badly they want to be winners. A player cannot afford to think about pain or the score or the weather or the coach. He has to think about winning. All the time. I only wish I had ten more years with Coach Lombardi. I'm afraid I might lose that edge he instilled. I find myself thinking about trying harder, and I don't think it's something you should force yourself to remember. He was the greatest man I ever knew, and I'm thankful he chose to work with me."

The season was done, and the Redskins had finished second behind Dallas in the Capitol Division of the Eastern Conference. Of the eight teams in the two Eastern Conference divisions, the Washington record was third best, behind Dallas with 11–2–1 in the Capitol and Cleveland, 10–3–1, in the Century. It was a good year, especially for a team that had been 5–9 the year before, 5–6–3 the year before that.

The last game of the season was the 20–10 loss to Dallas. The Cowboys, already having clinched the divisional race, were going through the motions. They had no reason to fear a loss. They were going to meet Cleveland in an Eastern Conference playoff game a week from then, and this one was just for loosening up.

But they won, and Lombardi's final message to his team was one of anger and disappointment. He stormed into the dressing room underneath the Cotton Bowl and ordered the doors barred. He spoke to the team at length.

"He told us," said one of the players, "that he was ashamed of us as men. He said the Cowboys didn't come out to win the game, but that we weren't men enough to teach them a lesson. I think he had a point. Only he can be so intense, and he must expect his players to be that way. When they aren't, he feels let down, defeated."

Season's end as usual for Lombardi meant planning for the next season, getting ready for the college draft. Lombardi knew the direction he wanted his selections to take. "We need defense," he said. "We have a fairly sound offense, but we need more help for the defense. If this team is going to be built, it will have to be with the defense. There was more raw talent when I took over the Packers, but these players have more experience. I can make do with the offense."

The draft brought a defensive end, Bill Brundige, the defensive tackle Manuel Sistrunk, the defensive backs James Harris and Paul Johnson, Jim Kates, linebacker, and Earl Maxfield, defensive tackle. Trading off the defensive tackle Frank Bosch, the Redskins got a linebacker, Dennis Gaubatz, from Baltimore, a hitting, heady player with vast potential.

The veterans had gained a year's experience playing for Vince Lombardi, which, as Charley Taylor put it, "is worth five playing for anybody else." It was ready to happen. Lombardi was anxious for the 1970 season to begin. He thought his team had a chance. He thought he had a chance.

He didn't.

No Time Left

IT IS EVEN NOW DIFFICULT TO PICTURE VINCE LOMBARDI as anything but well.

He was in New York three or four times between the college player draft and the month of June for functions of the National Football League. There were owners' meetings. There was the thirty-five-hour session during which the merger of the leagues was endangered until a realignment could be worked out. There was also a trip to visit his parents, and a Fordham sports-award dinner.

The realignment was the major issue. Team representatives, including Lombardi and Edward Bennett Williams for the Redskins, gathered in the offices of the league. Commissioner Pete Rozelle ordered them to come to terms before he would allow them to leave. It was May 17, 1969, and the owners of the original NFL teams were trying to decide which three of their brothers would be shifted to the new American Conference, a move that would create two thirteen-team conferences. Much was at stake—not the least was money. And the infighting was hot and bitter.

In the end, Cleveland, Baltimore, and Pittsburgh joined the American Football Conference. As Wellington Mara of the Giants remembered: "The only reason I allowed Cleveland to leave our conference was because Vince was in Washington. That guaranteed a rivalry between the Giants and the Redskins. Once it became clear that the general mood of the men was to approve the shifting of Cleveland, I insisted that the Giants and Redskins be joined in the same division permanently. So did Vince. Without him there, I doubt if I would have voted approval for the switching of the Browns."

Despite the marathon nature of that May 17 meeting, Lombardi looked well. He appeared pleased with the hard, almost combative atmosphere of the sessions. "It was the original NFL people against the original AFL people," he said. "Each side wanted to get the best deal for itself. I kind of enjoyed those sessions. It was really hard bargaining."

The entry in the official NFL record manual, under the date May 17, 1969:

"Following two previous meetings and a nonstop thirty-five hour, forty-five minute session in New York City, Commissioner Rozelle announced that the Baltimore Colts, Cleveland Browns, and Pittsburgh Steelers had agreed to join the present ten AFL teams and form a thirteen-team American Conference in the National Football League in 1970. The remaining thirteen NFL teams would form the National Conference. Each would be realigned into three divisions, with the conference champions meeting each year in the Super Bowl. The thirteen American Conference teams voted unanimously to realign into the following three divisions: Central—Cincinnati, Cleveland, Houston, Pittsburgh; Eastern—Baltimore, Boston, Buffalo, Miami, New York Jets; Western—Denver, Kansas City, Oakland, San Diego."

The National Conference was realigned on January 16,

1970. According to the NFL manual: "One of five plans submitted by Commissioner Rozelle was drawn in a lottery. The divisions: Eastern—Dallas, New York Giants, Philadelphia, St. Louis, Washington; Central—Chicago, Detroit, Green Bay, Minnesota; Western—Atlanta, Los Angeles, New Orleans, San Francisco."

The Giants and the Redskins were together. But they would have been in any case, for in each of five plans proposed, Washington and New York were to be in the same division. "It was the only way we would agree to anything," Mara said. "I insisted on it."

Fans across the country hailed the realignment. There would be interconference games during the regular season that were, in effect, interleague games. The NFL schedule-makers—Mark Duncan and Jim Kensil—outdid themselves. They set up such games as New York vs. New York, Kansas City vs. Saint Louis, San Francisco vs. Oakland, Los Angeles vs. San Diego, Houston vs. Dallas, New York Giants vs. Boston, Miami vs. Atlanta, Miami vs. New Orleans. There would be divisional playoff games to decide conference winners, and finally the Super Bowl to arrive at a league champion. The most exciting and colorful season in the history of the NFL was anticipated.

Lombardi fretted. He wanted to be in a contending position, as he had been first in the Super Bowl. But his Redskins were not his Packers. They were not even expected to be the winners of the Eastern Division. The Cowboys were the class of the five teams, with Saint Louis and New York considered threats.

It was to be a season of even more intense dedication, for he would have to force his players to win. Lombardi suspected it might be even more difficult to establish a season record over .500, since this time other teams would be expecting stiffer opposition from the Redskins and would be ready for them. It promised to be a draining, difficult season.

As winter faded to spring, Vince Lombardi continued pushing himself, preparing the team for training camp. He spoke to several of his players, cajoled and threatened, planned and instructed. He viewed the rookies at a special early gathering, made notes, and talked with his assistants about the prospects of every one of them. He was determined to get the most out of summer camp, for it would be a long season, and his men had to be trained, educated, and motivated.

And then, in the middle of June, he began to have stomach pains. They started as cramps, and they were agonizing. The pain would lessen, then disappear, only to come again. Even then, Lombardi must have admitted to himself that these were no ordinary stabs of pain.

"Hurt is in the mind," Lombardi said throughout his coaching career, a dogma he had learned from his tough and self-disciplined father. "Hurt is in the mind." So Lombardi ignored the stomach pains. He forced them out of his mind.

Slowly, ominously, his bodily functions began to change. "I remember I saw him in June," Wellington Mara said, "and he told me it hurt. It wasn't like Vince."

Finally, at the urging of family and friends, Lombardi took time out to see his doctor. Barium tests and X-rays followed. Near the end of June, Lombardi was ordered to the Georgetown University Hospital in Washington for exploratory surgery. His problem was described as "some sort of lower intestinal blockage."

On June 27, surgery was performed. The surgeons removed a two-foot-long section of colon. They had found a tumor, and reported "it appeared to be benign."

On July 10 Vince went home, much weakened. He had lost weight. But his eyes still sparkled, and his voice was firm and deep and in command. "I'll beat this," he told Mara. "I'm gonna beat this thing."

But it raged within him, and he went back to the hospital. That was on July 27, one month after the first surgery. There was a second operation, and it confirmed everyone's worst fears. The tumor was not at all benign. It was a cancer—sarcoma—rapidly spreading, extremely virulent.

Neither cobalt treatments nor surgery could help. Through the month of August, Lombardi held on. He named Bill Austin as interim coach of the Redskins and instructed Harland Svare to handle the defense, telling them he would be back. No one disbelieved him but the doctors. If strength of will could have saved him, Lombardi would be alive today. But it was physical, a disease that rampaged through his bloodstream into his vital organs.

The exhibition-game season opened, and the Redskins were stumbling.

Jim Norton, a defensive tackle, left camp. "I can't stand it," he said. "I can't concentrate on anything. I don't see how anyone else could. I have to get away."

Bill Austin fought to keep the players concentrating on football. "The atmosphere in camp was unbelievable," he remembers. "We'd walk around with our heads down, depressed and upset, thinking about Vince and not about the games. I can't blame any of them. I had to force myself to think about football."

Wellington Mara, accompanying the Giants to Pittsburgh for a preseason game on August 28, told me that he and his wife, Ann, had been to see Vince that week. I asked how he was. Mara looked blank, then shook his head. "No," he said. "No hope."

A pilgrimage to Lombardi's hospital bed began. Packers, Redskins, Giants; clergymen who were his friends, such as the Reverend Benedict Dudley, the Giants' team chaplain; former classmates, such as Ed Franco, Leo Paquin, Alex Wojciechowicz; owners of other teams, officials of the league, business acquaintances, fans. Marie Lombardi remained at his bedside throughout, calm and poised.

Alex Webster, Frank Gifford, and Mara journeyed to Washington in the last week of August. "We stayed in the room only a few minutes," Webster recalled. "He was in and out of a coma. I am sure he recognized us, though. He smiled."

Father Dudley, a friend of thirty years, was a frequent visitor. "Once he reached out and took my hand," the chaplain remembered. "We stood that way for a moment. Then his eyes closed, and he was back in the coma."

On Wednesday, September 2, the doctors issued a final, hopeless bulletin. "Mr. Lombardi is suffering," it said, "from an extremely virulent form of cancer."

At 7:12 the next morning, Thursday, September 3, 1970, as the sun was flooding the nation's capital, Vince Lombardi died. He was fifty-seven years old.

Two days later, the Redskins played the Miami Dolphins in a preseason game in Tampa, Florida. The Dolphins had been unbeaten in four summer games, defeating San Francisco and Baltimore in two of those games.

But the Redskins, wanting this game for Vince, won, 26–21.

Lombardi's body was placed on view in the Gawler Funeral Home in Washington on September 4. Then it was moved to the Abbey Funeral Home in New York for viewing Saturday and Sunday. A private rosary was said Sunday evening.

On Labor Day, Monday, September 7, he was buried.

At eleven o'clock that morning in Saint Patrick's Cathedral on Fifth Avenue in New York, there was a Mass of Resurrection for Vince Lombardi. Terence Cardinal Cooke, Archbishop of New York, was the chief celebrant. Among the nine concelebrants were Bishop Aloysius Wysislo of Green Bay, Wisconsin; Father Dudley; and the Reverend Monsignor Jeremiah Memecek, who had officiated at the marriage of Vince and Marie Lombardi on August 30, 1940.

More than three thousand persons attended the mass at Saint Patrick's. A thousand more crowded the sidewalks outside. Among those present were the six surviving members of the Seven Blocks of Granite; Robert Finch, representing President Nixon; Mrs. Robert F. Kennedy, Commissioner Rozelle, Phil Bengtson, Alex Webster, Bill Austin, Tom Landry, Norm Van Brocklin, Weeb Ewbank, Emlen Tunnell, and representatives of virtually every team in the NFL, including Philip Iselin of the Jets, Sid Gillman of the San Diego Chargers, Tex Schramm of the Dallas Cowboys, George Halas, Sr., and George Halas, Jr., of the Chicago Bears, and, of course, Dominick Olejniczak of the Packers. Mayor Donald Tilleman of Green Bay was also there, as well as a party of about fifty Packer players, coaches, and members of the board of directors, who had come in by a chartered flight. Another plane had brought in eighty-five players and members of the Washington Redskins' organization. In addition, there were twenty-five Giants' players, coaches, and front-office people.

In his eulogy Cardinal Cooke said: "Vince Lombardi was not only a sports celebrity, a great football coach marked for the Hall of Fame. What is ultimately more important than all is that he was a man of deep faith and firm hope."

The eulogy Bart Starr delivered struck a personal note:

"Coach Lombardi was a complex man. One minute he could be sky high with laughter and enthusiasm; the next, sullen and withdrawn in disgust. He remarked on numerous occasions that his greatest weakness was his lack of patience. Those of us who worked with him felt his impulsive wrath only to be comforted later with a sincere apology. The quality we'll remember most, though, has to be the magnificent leadership he displayed. The noblest form of leadership is through example. The finest example of leadership this country has known for some time was Vince Lombardi.

"The shouting, encouragement, inspirational messages, and vindictive assault on mistakes transcended the walls of our dressing rooms. In the privacy of those same rooms to have known a bigger man, kneeling in tearful prayer with his players after both triumph and defeat, was a strengthening experience that only his squads can ever fully appreciate.

"The scoreboard clock shows no time left—but make no mistake about it—Coach Lombardi didn't lose this game, it merely wasn't long enough."

President Nixon also sent a message of eulogy. And there was a noon mass concurrent with the services in New York at Saint Matthew's Cathedral in Washington.

The honorary pallbearers included Earl Blaik, Willie Davis, Paul Hornung, Bart Starr, Edward Bennett Williams, and presidents of the NFL teams.

There were thirty limousines in the funeral cortege that made the somber forty-one mile journey to Middletown, New Jersey. There in the Mount Olivet Cemetery Vince Lombardi was buried.

"God must be in terrible trouble," Jerry Kramer told Marie Lombardi, "if he needs Vince."

It was a day for remembering.

"I loved him," said George Halas, Sr., president of the Chicago Bears and founder of the NFL. "I loved him as a friend, as a man. When we met someplace, we would embrace each other. That seems sort of unusual for a couple of grown men, doesn't it? I only regret that we were friends, real friends, for only about five years. I wish it had been twenty-five. Or thirty-five. After his first operation, he and I met in New York. He said to me: 'You know about this thing, don't you, George? They took out only what they saw. Whatever happens now— well, it will happen. I am not afraid for myself. I am only afraid about the responsibilities I might leave the others.' "

Willie Davis, the all-pro defensive end now a successful Los Angeles businessman, remembered one day particularly. "It hadn't been one of our better days," he said, "even though we had won. The Coach stood in the middle of the locker room challenging us with those flashing eyes of his. He told us nobody wanted to pay the price to win as much as he did. He went on in that vein, testing us, feeling us out to see if the guys sitting there had enough inside them to make them feel the way he did. You could have heard a pin drop in that place. Then up stood Forrest Gregg to shout: 'Coach, I want to win.' I was leaning back on a stool in front of my locker, and just as Gregg finished, I lost my balance and made an awful commotion as I fell into my locker. Now you could really hear a pin drop, and Lombardi looked right through me with that intense look he reserved for times like this. Then, without knowing why, I jumped to my feet and stammered: 'I want to win, too.' "

Norb Hecker, who had been an assistant coach at Green Bay and the head coach at Atlanta, and who was now with the Giants, spoke for many: "After the funeral I looked at the coffin, and I said: 'He's not in there. That's an empty coffin.' If anyone was going to live forever, he's the guy. He'll never be dead in my mind. To me he's still coaching. Still the Coach. I can see him still, out there in that T-shirt and those baggy pants, like knickers, with that whistle around his neck and the sunglasses and baseball cap on."

That weekend, before a Redskins' preseason game against Baltimore, a tape was played over the public-address system at Robert F. Kennedy Stadium. Recorded weeks before he died, it served as Vince Lombardi's farewell. The voice still had its resonance as the words rolled across the field and echoed from the walls.

"I owe most everything to football, which I spent the greater part of my life in, and I have never lost my respect and my admiration, nor my love, for what I consider a great game. And each Sunday after the battle, one group savors victory, another group lives in the bitterness of defeat. The many hurts seem a small price to pay for having won, and there is no reason at all that is adequate for having lost. The winner— to the winner there is one hundred percent elation, one hundred percent laughter, one hundred percent fun. And to the loser—the only thing left for him is a one hundred percent resolution, and a one hundred percent determination. As a game, I think football is a great deal like life and that it demands a man's personal commitment toward excellence, and toward victory, even though you know that ultimate victory can never be completely won, that it must be pursued with all of one's might. And each week there's a new encounter and each year a new challenge. But all of the money and all the color, all of the display—they linger only in the memory. But the spirit, the will to win, and the will to excel—these are the things that endure. And these are the qualities, of course, that are so much more important than any of the events that occasion them. And I would like to say that the quality of any man's life has got to be a full measure of that man's personal commitment to excellence and to victory, regardless of what field he may be in."

THE LOMBARDI RECORD

Green Bay Packers

1959

Green Bay 9, Chicago 6
Green Bay 28, Detroit 10
Green Bay 21, San Francisco 20
Los Angeles 45, Green Bay 6
Baltimore 38, Green Bay 21
New York 20, Green Bay 3
Chicago 28, Green Bay 17

Baltimore 28, Green Bay 24
Green Bay 21, Washington 0
Green Bay 24, Detroit 17
Green Bay 38, Los Angeles 20
Green Bay 36, San Francisco 14

Won 7, Lost 5

1960

Chicago 17, Green Bay 14
Green Bay 28, Detroit 9
Green Bay 35, Baltimore 21
Green Bay 41, San Francisco 14
Green Bay 19, Pittsburgh 13
Baltimore 38, Green Bay 24
Green Bay 41, Dallas 7

Los Angeles 33, Green Bay 31
Detroit 23, Green Bay 10
Green Bay 41, Chicago 13
Green Bay 13, San Francisco 0
Green Bay 35, Los Angeles 21

Won 8, Lost 4

NFL CHAMPIONSHIP   Philadelphia 17, Green Bay 13

1961

Detroit 17, Green Bay 13
Green Bay 30, San Francisco 10
Green Bay 24, Chicago 0
Green Bay 45, Baltimore 7
Green Bay 49, Cleveland 17
Green Bay 33, Minnesota 7
Green Bay 28, Minnesota 10
Baltimore 45, Green Bay 21

Green Bay 31, Chicago 28
Green Bay 35, Los Angeles 17
Green Bay 17, Detroit 9
Green Bay 20, New York 17
San Francisco 22, Green Bay 21
Green Bay 24, Los Angeles 17

Won 11, Lost 3

NFL CHAMPIONSHIP   Green Bay 37, New York 0

1962

Green Bay 34, Minnesota 7
Green Bay 17, Saint Louis 0
Green Bay 49, Chicago 0
Green Bay 9, Detroit 7
Green Bay 48, Minnesota 21
Green Bay 31, San Francisco 13
Green Bay 17, Baltimore 6
Green Bay 38, Chicago 7

Green Bay 49, Philadelphia 0
Green Bay 17, Baltimore 13
Detroit 26, Green Bay 14
Green Bay 41, Los Angeles 10
Green Bay 31, San Francisco 21
Green Bay 20, Los Angeles 17

Won 13, Lost 1

NFL CHAMPIONSHIP

Green Bay 16, New York 7

1963

Chicago 10, Green Bay 3
Green Bay 31, Detroit 10
Green Bay 31, Baltimore 20
Green Bay 42, Los Angeles 10
Green Bay 37, Minnesota 28
Green Bay 30, Saint Louis 7
Green Bay 34, Baltimore 20
Green Bay 33, Pittsburgh 14

Green Bay 24, Minnesota 7
Chicago 26, Green Bay 7
Green Bay 28, San Francisco 10
Green Bay 13, Detroit 13 (tie)
Green Bay 31, Los Angeles 14
Green Bay 21, San Francisco 17

Won 11, Lost 2, Tied 1

1964

Green Bay 23, Chicago 12
Baltimore 21, Green Bay 20
Green Bay 14, Detroit 10
Minnesota 24, Green Bay 23
Green Bay 24, San Francisco 14
Baltimore 24, Green Bay 21
Los Angeles 27, Green Bay 17
Green Bay 42, Minnesota 13

Green Bay 30, Detroit 7
San Francisco 24, Green Bay 14
Green Bay 28, Cleveland 21
Green Bay 45, Dallas 21
Green Bay 17, Chicago 3
Green Bay 24, Los Angeles 24 (tie)

Won 8, Lost 5, Tied 1

1965

Green Bay 41, Pittsburgh 9
Green Bay 20, Baltimore 17
Green Bay 23, Chicago 14
Green Bay 27, San Francisco 10
Green Bay 31, Detroit 21
Green Bay 13, Dallas 3
Chicago 31, Green Bay 10
Detroit 12, Green Bay 7

Green Bay 6, Los Angeles 3
Green Bay 38, Minnesota 13
Los Angeles 21, Green Bay 10
Green Bay 24, Minnesota 19
Green Bay 42, Baltimore 27
Green Bay 24, San Francisco 24 (tie)

Won 10, Lost 3, Tied 1

Western Conference Playoff

Green Bay 13, Baltimore 10

NFL CHAMPIONSHIP

Green Bay 23, Cleveland 12

1966

Green Bay 24, Baltimore 3
Green Bay 21, Cleveland 20
Green Bay 24, Los Angeles 13
Green Bay 23, Detroit 14
San Francisco 21, Green Bay 20
Green Bay 17, Chicago 0
Green Bay 56, Atlanta 3
Green Bay 31, Detroit 7

Minnesota 20, Green Bay 17
Green Bay 13, Chicago 6
Green Bay 28, Minnesota 16
Green Bay 20, San Francisco 7
Green Bay 14, Baltimore 10
Green Bay 27, Los Angeles 23

Won 12, Lost 2

NFL CHAMPIONSHIP   Green Bay 34, Dallas 27

SUPER BOWL I   Green Bay 35, Kansas City 10

1967

Green Bay 17, Detroit 17 (tie)
Green Bay 13, Chicago 10
Green Bay 23, Atlanta 0
Green Bay 27, Detroit 17
Minnesota 10, Green Bay 7
Green Bay 48, New York 21
Green Bay 31, Saint Louis 23
Baltimore 13, Green Bay 10

Green Bay 55, Cleveland 7
Green Bay 13, San Francisco 0
Green Bay 17, Chicago 13
Green Bay 30, Minnesota 27
Los Angeles 27, Green Bay 24
Pittsburgh 24, Green Bay 17

Won 9, Lost 4, Tied 1

Western Conference Playoff   Green Bay 28, Los Angeles 7

NFL CHAMPIONSHIP   Green Bay 21, Dallas 17
SUPER BOWL II   Green Bay 33, Oakland 14

Washington Redskins

1969

Washington 26, New Orleans 20
Cleveland 27, Washington 23
Washington 17, San Francisco 17
   (tie)
Washington 33, Saint Louis 17
Washington 20, New York 14
Washington 14, Pittsburgh 7
Baltimore 41, Washington 17

Washington 28, Philadelphia 28
   (tie)
Dallas 41, Washington 28
Washington 27, Atlanta 20
Los Angeles 24, Washington 13
Washington 34, Philadelphia 29
Washington 17, New Orleans 14
Dallas 20, Washington 10
Won 7, Lost 5, Tied 2

THE LOMBARDI ROSTERS

Green Bay Packers, 1959–1967

Herb Adderley, defensive back
Ben Agajanian, place-kicker
Lionel Aldridge, defensive end
Bill Anderson, tight end
Donnie Anderson, running back
Gary Barnes, wide receiver
Jan Barrett, wide receiver
Ken Beck, tackle
Tom Bettis, linebacker
Ed Blaine, guard
Nate Borden, running back
Ken Bowman, center
Dave Bradley, guard
Zeke Bratkowski, quarterback
Gene Breen, linebacker
Allen Brown, wide receiver
Tim Brown, running back
Tom Brown, defensive back
Bill Butler, running back
Lee Roy Caffey, linebacker
Dick Capp, linebacker
Lew Carpenter, running back, wide receiver
Don Chandler, place-kicker
Dennis Claridge, quarterback
Junior Coffey, running back
Tommy Joe Crutcher, linebacker
Dan Currie, linebacker
Bill Curry, linebacker, center
Andy Cvercko, guard
Carroll Dale, wide receiver
Ben Davidson, defensive end
Willie Davis, defensive end
Bobby Dillon, running back
John Dittrich, guard
Boyd Dowler, wide receiver
Jim Flanagan, linebacker
Marv Fleming, tight end
Lee Folkins, wide receiver
Bill Forrester, linebacker
Joe Francis, running back
Bob Freeman, running back

Ron Gassert, tackle
Gale Gillingham, guard
Jim Grabowski, running back
Forrest Gregg, tackle
Hank Gremminger, defensive back
Dan Grimm, guard
Earl Gros, running back
Dale Hackbart, defensive back
Dave Hanner, defensive tackle
Doug Hart, defensive back
Dave Hathcock, defensive back
Ken Haycraft, wide receiver
Urban Henry, tackle
Larry Hickman, running back
Don Horn, quarterback
Paul Hornung, running back, place-
   kicker
Bob Hyland, tackle, center
Ken Iman, linebacker
Allen Jacobs, running back
Claudis James, wide receiver
Bob Jeter, defensive back
Henry Jordan, defensive tackle
Gary Knalfelc, tight end
Ron Kostelnik, defensive tackle
Jerry Kramer, guard
Ron Kramer, tight end
Bob Long, wide receiver
John McDowell, guard
Lamar McHan, quarterback
Max McGee, wide receiver
Don McIlhenny, running back
Red Mack, running back
Rich Marshall, tackle
Norm Masters, tackle
Steve Meilinger, wide receiver
Chuck Mercein, running back
Frank Mestnik, running back
John Miller, tackle
Tom Moore, running back
Ray Nitschke, linebacker
Jerry Norton, defensive back

Dick Pesonen, defensive back
Elijah Pitts, running back
Bill Quinlan, defensive end
Jim Ringo, center
John Roach, quarterback
Dave Robinson, linebacker
John Rowser, defensive back
Bob Skoronski, tackle
Bart Starr, quarterback
John Symank, defensive back
Jim Taylor, running back
Jim Temp, wide receiver
Fred Thurston, guard

Nelson Toburen, linebacker
Emlen Tunnell, defensive back
Phil Vandersea, linebacker
Lloyd Voss, defensive tackle
Jim Weatherwax, defensive tackle
Jesse Whittenton, defensive back
A.D. Williams, wide receiver
Howard Williams, running back
Travis Williams, running back
Ben Wilson, running back
Paul Winslow, wide receiver
Willie Wood, defensive back
Steve Wright, tackle

Washington Redskins, 1969

Gerry Allen, running back
Mike Bass, defensive back
Gary Beban, quarterback, wide receiver
Frank Bosch, defensive tackle
Mike Bragg, place-kicker
Larry Brown, running back
Tom Brown, defensive back
Bob Brunet, running back
Leo Carroll, defensive end
Dennis Crane, defensive tackle, offensive tackle
Dave Crossan, center
John Didion, center, linebacker
Steve Duich, guard
Henry Dyer, running back
Eugene Epps, wide receiver, defensive back
Pat Fischer, defensive back
Charlie Gogolak, place-kicker
Dan Grimm, guard
Chris Hanburger, linebacker
Charlie Harraway, running back
Rickie Harris, defensive back
Len Hauss, center
John Hoffman, defensive end
Sam Huff, linebacker
Sonny Jurgensen, quarterback
Carl Kammerer, defensive end

Curt Knight, place-kicker
Dave Kopay, running back
Bob Long, wide receiver
Dave Long, defensive end
John Love, wide receiver
Marlin McKeever, linebacker
Harold McLinton, linebacker
Chuck Mercein, running back
Jim Norton, defensive tackle
Brig Owens, defensive back
Vince Promuto, guard
Pat Richter, tight end, place-kicker
Walt Roberts, wide receiver
Walt Rock, tackle
Tom Roussel, linebacker
Frank Ryan, quarterback
Ray Schoenke, tackle
Bob Shannon, wide receiver
Jerry Smith, tight end
Jim Snowden, tackle
Fred Sumrall, defensive tackle
Danny Talbott, quarterback
Charley Taylor, wide receiver
Harry Theofilides, quarterback
Ted Vactor, defensive back
Bob Wade, defensive back
A.D. Whitfield, running back
John Wooten, guard

INDEX